How to Deal With Difficult People

Learn to Get Along With People You Can't Stand, and Bring Out Their Best

By: Dave Young

ALL RIGHTS RESERVED

No part of this book may be reproduced, stored in a retrieval system, or transmitted in any form or by any means, electronic, mechanical, photocopying, recording, scanning, or otherwise, without the prior written permission of the publisher.

Limit of Liability/Disclaimer of Warranty: the publisher and the author make no representations or warranties with respect to the accuracy or completeness of the contents of this work and specifically disclaim all warranties, including without limitation warranties of fitness for a particular purpose. No warranty may be created or extended by sales or promotional materials. The advice and strategies contained herein may not be suitable for every situation. This work is sold with the understanding that the publisher is not engaged in rendering medical, legal or other professional advice or services. If professional assistance is required, the services of a competent professional person should be sought. Neither the publisher nor the author shall be liable for damages arising herefrom. The fact that an individual, organization or website is referred to in this work as a citation and/or potential source of further information does not mean that the author or the publisher endorses the information the individuals, organization or website may provide or recommendations they/it may make. Further, readers should be aware that websites listed on this work may have changed or disappeared between when this work was written and when it is read.

Table of Contents

Introduction 4

Chapter 1 Identifying a Difficult Person 7

Chapter 2 Dealing with Difficult People in the Workplace 11

Chapter 3 Dealing with Difficult People in the Family 20

Chapter 4 Dealing with Difficult Parents 27

Chapter 5 Dealing with Difficult In-Laws 37

Chapter 6 Dealing with Difficult Spouses 43

Chapter 7 Dealing with Difficult Children 53

Chapter 8 Dealing with Difficult Teens 64

Chapter 9 Dealing with Difficult People as a Whole 79

Chapter 10 Coping Strategies for Dealing with Difficult People 86

Chapter 12 Encouraging Yourself to Be Your Best 97

Chapter 13 Encouraging Others to Be Their Best 106

Chapter 14 Understanding Trauma 112

Chapter 15 Healing Yourself 121

Conclusion 126

Introduction

If you have picked up a copy of this book, you are more than aware of the fact that we live in a society filled with individuals who are difficult to get along with. Difficult people are those whom we just can't seem to get along with, for whatever underlying reason that may be. In this book, we will be exploring the world of difficult people, and how you can learn to not only get along with people that you just cannot stand but also bring out their best as well!

Let's first dive into why learning how to deal with difficult people is important in virtually any situation. For starters, effectively dealing with difficult people can, in turn, give you a positive upper hand. Difficult people can be found all around you, from next-door neighbors to teachers, in-laws, employers, coworkers, and even wait staff. And whether their difficult behavior is something that is in their nature, or whether they may just be having a bad day, effectively reading people's behavior is the best way to readjust yourself to cope with the situation and handle it properly.

Learning such techniques may prove to be a daunting task, but the more you are able to study them, the easier they will be to implement into your daily life. These strategies will additionally be able to assist you in handling difficult individuals no matter who they are or where you end up coming across them. It is of the utmost importance to learn to implement these strategies carefully and keep at them. Change is undoubtedly one of the most difficult things that we have to go through in our lives, and it can be incredibly hard to do so.

To expand on that thought, it is even more difficult to try and change others, especially if they are already difficult in nature.

The key to really learning how to deal with difficult people is to understand that it is OK to *not* understand why they are the way they are. From past trauma to the inability to cope and handle social situations, there are many reasons why people become "difficult" in their nature. The more you can come to understand this fact, the easier it will be to accept them as they are, and to potentially come to them from a place of love and acceptance, as tough as this may be at times.

Difficult people can be insanely hard to deal with, and if you have to deal with them on a regular basis it may be quite trying on your personal mental health and your overall sense of well-being. You need to ensure that you are taking care of yourself and putting yourself first and foremost for your own well-being. We will most certainly provide you with the proper steps and a plan of action to learn how to protect yourself and your mental state when it comes to dealing with difficult people, no matter who they are or how often you are forced to come in contact with them.

One thing that you may want to keep in mind as you read the following pages is that the people who are the most difficult to deal with can, in fact, be some of the most valuable teachers that you ever encounter. The trying issues that are related to them are not yours to carry, but how you control yourself when you are dealing with that difficult person most certainly plays a significant factor in the overall situation. When you learn how to be successful at dealing with a difficult person, you are also learning valuable and important lessons about yourself. You need to learn how to work on positively dealing with these individuals so that you can develop the necessary skills to overcome challenging situations with them.

People are who they were born to be. And difficult people are some of the hardest to coax to create positive change in their lives. You need to make sure that you do not strive to necessarily change, condemn, or judge someone, and instead try and look for their value. Sometimes a difficult person's value can get lost and hidden, but when you take the time to look past their barriers, you may just end up finding that the person really has a tremendous amount to offer.

This book will serve as a highly beneficial guide to help you get through some trying circumstances with some of the most difficult people in your life. Whether you are forced to deal with these individuals because they are friends, family, or coworkers, or if you work at a job where people are often highly demanding and difficult to deal with, we will be providing you with some of the top tips and effective strategies to help you get through virtually any situation. Let's get started!

Chapter 1
Identifying a Difficult Person

There are so many different personality types out there that it can all too often be quite hard to pinpoint who exactly is a "difficult person." In this first section, we will be exploring some of the different characteristics that tend to make up what is defined as a difficult person, in order to better be able to ascertain who those people are and how you can point them out before they end up robbing you of your sanity.

Most people who can be categorized as difficult seem to think that the world owes them something. These people tend to be overdramatic and are fueled by the reactions they get from those around them, and they feel the need to be the focal point of attention. They are often opinionated, egocentric, and narcissistic and are always the first ones to spill virtually every detail of their life, even if the only question asked is, "How was your weekend?" They will spare no shortage of details regarding their drama-filled story.

Difficult people are seemingly always seeking ways to get something in return for nothing. They are not compassionate individuals, but they are self-serving ones. If you ask a favor of them, they will be the first ones to remind you again and again that they did something for you, and they will inevitably find a way to hold it against you. If whatever it was that they did for you was not in any way in their own best interest, you can be sure that you will ultimately find yourself getting bullied into repaying them in a manner they see fit.

Difficult people also tend to remain stuck in the past and are always the ones who will readily play the victim. This goes back to their narcissistic attitude and their belief the world owes them something. Difficult individuals can utilize anything from family to illness to get whatever it is they want, and they are more than eager to manipulate those around them. They tend to live in the past and are constantly in a victimization mode, reeling those around them into their lives by making them feel sorry for them, and guilting them if they do not.

The most baffling part of all of this is that difficult people are, in fact, completely oblivious to the fact that they are doing these things or being difficult, which makes it equally difficult to confront those individuals about their behavior and how it is affecting those around them. They tend to live in their own world, keeping their heads in the sand and putting the blame on others about the situations they find themselves in. That is what makes difficult people so hard to get along with; they are in complete denial of what is happening around them or whom their behavior is adversely affecting, and even if they are aware of it, they really couldn't care less.

It should also be noted that you really need to tread lightly when you are dealing with difficult people. These individuals do not like confrontation and loathe having the tables turned on them when they find themselves no longer in charge of the situation at hand and the stories they are twisting. You will find that when these people get called out on their behavior, they will turn the opposite direction and take their negative attributes along to the next person whom they believe they can manipulate into feeling sorry for them and hearing what they have to say. Difficult people find their strength through manipulation, as it gives them a sense of control and power over things that perhaps they feel they are not really in control of.

When it comes to dealing with difficult people, you need to take the time to really recognize that they are difficult before you even try and engage with them, if at all possible. When you are capable of learning how to successfully recognize these individuals, you can take the right course of action to protect yourself against them. You also have the chance to process what they are doing and why they are doing it, and then talk them off the ledge or simply get them to back off from you so that you no longer have to even engage with them in the first place.

Difficult people can create a hard circumstance for you. It really is almost inevitable, but again, the more you learn how to identify them, the easier it will be to protect yourself in the long run. It is of the utmost importance to keep in mind as you read the following pages that you need to have a bit of patience, not necessarily for the difficult person whom you are dealing with, but for yourself. Dealing with difficult people is truly a learning curve that you need to adapt to in order to be successful overall. Learning new things takes time, and a tremendous amount of effort is needed in order to learn how to really adapt to a new way of living and understanding difficult people and overcoming situations and circumstances that involve them.

Difficult people are, as the name implies, difficult. Dealing with them in every sense of the word can all too often be unbearably hard to do. The good news, however, is that you can take back a sense of control for yourself and your own emotional well-being, and in the following chapters, we will show you precisely how to do that, from being able to effectively narrow down who is going to be a difficult person to learning how to implement effective strategies and unique tips to take on any situation. After reading the following chapters, you will find yourself a stronger, more confident individual who is ready to handle any situation that a difficult person may very well put you in the midst of.

Chapter 2
Dealing with Difficult People in the Workplace

To get started, it is pretty important to learn how to deal with difficult coworkers. There are a number of reasons why it is crucial to learn how to deal with coworkers and they will be discussed throughout this chapter.

One of the trickiest issues of learning how to get along with difficult individuals is figuring out how to do so within the confines of a work environment. Even if you absolutely love your job, it does not necessarily mean that you are going to get along with all of your colleagues. In fact, it has been noted that upward of approximately 80 percent of people in the workplace have experienced moderate to severe stress because they have had to collaborate with one or more difficult colleagues. That really is a striking number!

Regardless of why it is that you find someone difficult, it is crucial to your own professional and personal successes that you are at least somewhat capable of being able to work with anyone (whether you like it or not). If you allow the behavior of another person to get to you on a personal level in the workplace, your work will undoubtedly suffer. This is important for a number of reasons:

    A. You see them every day.
    B. You deserve a stress-free workday.
    C. Your job may depend on it.

There are a couple of issues to think about when it comes to ultimately choosing how you want to handle dealing with difficult people in the workplace. One thing to consider is that you may be missing out on a tremendous amount of learning from them if you opt to avoid them altogether, and you may end up being seen as "difficult" to work with as well. While it is a great thing to get along with all of your coworkers, even on the best days, it just is not a realistic expectation. What you can do, however, is practice effective strategies for being able to work and collaborate with difficult coworkers. Here are some of the top tips that you may want to consider implementing:

- **Check yourself.** First and foremost, evaluate yourself before putting the blame entirely on someone else. Often, we get a bad taste in our mouths from someone because we are reminded of someone else whom we didn't like in the past. If the difficult coworker reminds you of someone from your past that you just didn't get along with or who wronged you in some type of way, you need to acknowledge this and remind yourself that your coworker is not that person. It may just help you learn how to push past whatever it is about them that bothers you.
- **Ignore or avoid them.** This may sound like your mother's run-of-the-mill advice, but if you can avoid the coworker that is difficult to be around or work with, do it. You do not have to be rude or inconsiderate to the individual; you can be polite while also setting your boundaries. If you do not have to work closely with or associate with the difficult person on a regular basis, save yourself the stress and hassle and avoid them.

- **Avoid getting personal.** You need to take the high road when it comes to your career and someone who threatens to bring you down. Do not allow yourself to get baited into gossip, rivalry, or unprofessional conduct; be sure to remain professional at all times, no matter what. If you are having issues with someone in the workplace and it is becoming personal in terms of verbal put-downs, threats, or other negative comments, you need to inform a superior before things go too far and you end up in a really bad situation.
- **Communicate.** Your irritating or difficult coworkers may just be completely oblivious to the fact that they are even bothering you. Open a line of communication by phrasing whatever it is that is upsetting you, but be cautious that you are not hurtful or accusatory. When you open those lines of communication, both parties have the opportunity to express themselves equally and potentially find a middle ground for being able to resolve the issue. You may end up being able to not only help each other, out but also tolerate that individual.
- **Remind yourself.** It is of the utmost importance to take the time to remind yourself of what you stand to gain in your career. This is particularly important if you can actually learn something from your difficult coworker and, in turn, produce some really good work together. If you can put your best foot forward and keep reminding yourself of how you can leverage your collaboration, you can end up reaping the rewards in your professional career.

- **Ask for help.** If you have exhausted all of your other options—from trying to ignore or avoid the difficult coworker to actively communicating with them and trying to get along and collaborate with them—and you just are not able to get through the issue on your own, you may need to voice your concerns to a superior. Even documenting the issue can protect you in the future in the event that anything negative ever happens between you and your coworker. Try and use this as a last resort, however, as you do not want to seem too eager to cause discord within your place of work if it doesn't have to go that way.

Dealing with a difficult colleague can be one of the most trying things that you have to deal with in your professional career, but the good news is that you do not have to sit back and continuously allow that person to unnerve you. It is important to stand up for yourself in your place of business, to speak up when you need to, and to not be afraid to ask for help if you need it.

Even more challenging than dealing with a difficult coworker or colleague in the workplace is the very pressing issue of having to deal with a difficult boss. Let's go over an example of a scenario where dealing with a difficult boss can get a bit tricky.

A good friend of mine was once working for a company that she genuinely enjoyed. She was the administrative assistant, and she was great at her job—always smiling, always polite (even to the most difficult clients), and ready to help wherever needed. The only issue she had was having to deal with a very difficult boss who often brought her down. She would always arrive on time, make coffee for the office, prepare the conference room for the day's meetings and activities, and vacuum and tidy up her front office desk area and the waiting lobby. Then she would sit down to get her day started by checking emails and messages. Sure, every day was pretty standard and routine, but she liked it.

Unfortunately, when her boss came in about an hour or so after her, a dark cloud would pass through the lobby. He was the type of man that you could tell very likely had a good heart, but he piled so much on himself in the personal and professional sense that anyone who crossed his path would become the immediate target for his grievances and annoyances. There was virtually nothing she, or anyone else in the office, could seemingly do right. And he would immediately be there to call them out on their faults, but never to applaud them on their successes. It was upsetting and defeating for her, to say the very least. But she loved her coworkers and loved her job, and let's be honest: she desperately needed the paycheck. So what could she do?

Well, she took it upon herself to reach out to some of her trusted coworkers, not to gossip, but to honestly ask if they felt as personally attacked as she did, and she was met with enthusiastic agreement. The people who worked in that office felt personally attacked and belittled and were made to feel less than their best by their boss—not just on certain occasions, but daily. They decided that the time had finally come where they needed to address how they were feeling and to bring it up to their boss in a nice, respectful manner, but almost in an intervention sort of way.

Again, they knew that their boss had a good heart, and that he would listen to what they had to say regarding how they felt about how he was treating them, but would he be open to change? My friend told her boss that the other employees had concerns about an issue that had arisen in the office and they wanted to arrange a time to sit down and meet with him. He of course was immediately concerned, so he arranged for a time later that afternoon to sit down with everyone.

They all met in the conference room at the previously arranged time, and it was my friend who spoke up first to inform him what the meeting was to entail and why they were concerned with regards to what was happening in the office. She explained the treatment that the employees felt was unfair and completely unnecessary. The boss listened to their concerns with empathy, apologized, and stated that he would make the necessary attempts to ensure that he changed his attitude toward them. And he did.

Unfortunately, this was not the end of the bad treatment. He made attempts, sure, but he could not entirely change what had become such a reliable characteristic for him. He felt that treating people in the manner he did had led him to success and power within the organization. Another unfortunate fact was that the company was a nonprofit organization that did not have a human resources department the employees could turn to for additional assistance or any sense of guidance or direction. What they did have, however, was a board of directors who met monthly, and every quarter the employees had the opportunity to fill out an evaluation regarding how the boss was doing as the leader of the organization.

Mind you, the evaluation was the final straw. The employees had met with their boss two more times following the initial meeting and expressed their concerns over the fact that the treatment they were receiving was simply not improving. Sure, he had his OK days, but they were few and far between, and the employees had had enough of their difficult boss. The employees met with each other in order to express their concerns and get a general consensus of whether filling out the evaluation and expressing their concerns to the board of directors would be the best thing to do. They all agreed it was, and the board of directors received their evaluations.

The board of directors opted to speak privately and individually with the members of the company who had voiced their concerns in the evaluation in order to confirm all of their stories and issues and to get a better sense of how they had been treated. Interestingly enough, the board of directors had taken issue with the difficult boss as well. They met with the boss in order to come up with a proper solution and confirm the fact that the employees had made multiple attempts at expressing their issues with his treatment of them and had requested that his behavior change.

He admitted that all of it was true and that while he had made several attempts to change and modify his behavior, he was simply not successful in doing so. He was having some personal issues at home, and that was heavily weighing on his behavior when he came into the office. He informed the board of directors that he wanted to meet with the employees and the board of directors in order to determine what solutions would be necessary to resolve the situation.

The meeting went well. Everything was laid out on the table in a clear, concise, and direct manner, and there was no finger-pointing. It became apparent that he was simply dealing with personal issues that were beyond his emotional capacity, and he agreed to seek personal counseling from a licensed professional as opposed to taking a "warning" and trying to fix things on his own. He was a difficult person, yes, but he also wanted help to fix himself. He no longer wanted to treat people in the manner he was, and he acknowledged that his issues were hurting not only people in the office but also outside associates, and even his own family.

That is the one of the most complicated areas of dealing with difficult people. You just never know who is emotionally suffering and lashing out at those around them because they can't process their internal pain on their own.

My friend and her coworkers were able to successfully resolve the situation, but it took time and a tremendous amount of effort on their part. However, they knew that he was a genuinely good person and they wanted to not only resolve the issue but help someone they really cared about, despite his difficult personality.

My friend has since changed companies, but only because she ended up moving out of state and getting a better position. She still asserts that while that was easily one of the most trying times of her professional life, she learned a number of things about dealing with difficult people, especially when it comes to that difficult person being your boss. It can be incredibly hard to try and address these issues, particularly if you are not an outspoken person. However, you should never allow yourself to be put into situations where you are not comfortable; where you are met with issues of anger or heavy stress on a consistent basis; or where you are with someone who belittles, is condescending, or is harassing you in any sort of way.

Help can be found in your place of business. Whether it is a board of directors, as was the case with my friend, a human resources department, your actual boss (if you are dealing with issues related to your coworkers or colleagues), or other employees who may be having similar issues as well. Even if you are not comfortable speaking up and speaking out, it may very well come down to that. And you need to make sure that you document the situations by reporting them to someone you trust—for example, a boss, the board of directors, or a human resources department—in order to avoid bigger issues down the road.

Eleanor Roosevelt once said that "no one can make you feel inferior without your consent." You need to keep that in mind when you are dealing with difficult people. It really does not matter who it is— it could be a coworker or someone in a higher position in your company—no one should make you feel like you are not a valid individual who is more than deserving of being treated like a decent human being.

If you are receiving anything less than that, especially at your place of work, you need to take matters into your own hands and speak up for yourself. Be proud of who you are and your capabilities, and never let a difficult person steal your happiness and level of comfort away from you.

Chapter 3
Dealing with Difficult People in the Family

Realistically speaking, the only people who are more difficult to deal with outside of the workplace are often within your very own family. Whether it's siblings, in-laws, a spouse, or other family members, dealing with difficult people who are close to you can be one of the most pressing and hard issues that you will have to face in your life. We will touch on how to deal with parents, in-laws, and spouses more in-depth in their own individual chapters, but here I wanted to provide you with some general, helpful information that can be used for dealing with basically any family member. There are a lot of things that you can do to strategize and potentially be able to resolve the underlying issues at hand.

The biggest thing is to open the lines of communication between individuals. This is the principal step because if you are dealing with a difficult person who is close to you, whether a friend, family member, or in-law, these people are close to you for a reason. If you don't get along with your husband's mother, that is a huge issue that is going to ultimately affect your marriage. If you don't get along with one of your siblings, that can have an impact on the rest of your family as a whole.

For example, a very good friend of mine grew up close to his siblings. He had four sisters in total from a "his, hers, and ours" type of blended family. He was the "baby boy" and very much favored by his father. Over the years his family would grow apart in terms of distance, but not love. He would eventually move with his own family back to his original home state in order to be closer to his father and a few other relatives from his dad's side of the family. That year he had some of the best moments of his life, and he had a wonderful time getting to share small-town life with his new wife and young son, while also making great memories with his dad, whom he had been apart from for a good ten years.

    Unfortunately, that time would abruptly come to a screeching halt with the sudden passing of his father via an unexpected accident that would forever change the structure of his entire family, particularly concerning his relationship with his oldest sister. With their father in the hospital, the sister was notified of the accident and immediately flew up to be with the rest of the family while their dad was clinging to life. He would eventually be taken off life support, and my friend, being the eldest male, and his older sister were immediately thrown into the chaos of things that follow a death in the family: wills, trusts, anger, grief, burial decisions, and final payments and arrangements. It is more than virtually anyone can process in such a short amount of time.

    My friend noticed that throughout this process of finalizing everything and getting things in order, his sister appeared to slowly be losing it. She was grieving, but at the same time, she was refusing to listen to anything my friend was trying to say or help her with. She was doing things like trying to break into their dad's safe to get the money that my friend knew was not even there in the first place. She had to get to the bank to immediately withdraw the funds and close accounts. Everything was becoming about money, and that was incredibly alarming to him. She was not allowing herself to process the grief that she was experiencing, and her actions were tearing their entire family apart.

She would end up stealing the truck that belonged to my friend's father and was willed to him, along with the ashes of their dad. My friend and his family were forced to move into his father's home to care for the home and the large amounts of property that were tied to it in order to protect and maintain everything until the home could sell. Once the sister returned to her own home several states away, she continued to harass my friend regarding everything, from demanding that he move out to demanding his signature for things he had been told by the lawyer not to sign. She had lost her senses and was lashing out at everyone around her in grief and anger.

Two years later, the two are not on speaking terms. He is still living on the property because she refuses to have a conversation with him and their younger sister. The trust of the father's estate was to be divided between the three of them, but because of her difficult nature, nothing can get accomplished in accordance with their father's will and wishes.

I can give you example after example of certain situations that are just like this, from a death in the family that causes people to become money hungry and self-centered, to siblings who have a falling-out over who mom's favorite is, to overprotective and invasive mothers-in-law.

When it comes to dealing with issues that are related to family members, trying to figure out the best resolution is something that needs to be approached on a case-by-case basis. You really cannot determine why difficult people are acting a certain way about any given situation. But issues that involve difficult family members can often be resolved when all parties that are involved are willing to communicate and genuinely hear what one another has to say. Unfortunately, that is all too often incredibly hard to do when you are dealing with difficult people, regardless of the family relation or what the issue is at hand.

Whoever it is that you are having issues with is somehow close to you, and that should be cause enough to desire to fix or try to somewhat resolve the underlying issue. Whether it is for yourself, your spouse, or other members of your family, figuring out a proper solution to resolve the issue is going to be the first and most important step you can take to get along with that person, and maybe even find a way to bring out the best in both of you for the good of your family and those around you.

The first thing you need to do is sit with yourself to decide what it is that really bothers you about the individual in the first place. Is it something simple that you can just get past? Or is it something deeper that is really bothering you and you just can't let go? When you can finally narrow down what the underlying issue is, you can then decide the best course of action to take and sit down and verbalize your issue, or issues, to the difficult person.

Next, you need to determine if you need to bring your issues about that person up to a third party who may potentially be "caught in the middle" of it all. This is particularly important if your issue has to do with your in-laws. If your spouse is close to their family, you are not going to want to corner that difficult person and start telling them all of the issues you have with them. That is going to come back and really hit you hard. The same thing goes for a member of your own family as well; if you are having issues with a parent or sibling, your best offense is going to be a good defense. You don't necessarily have to side with that third-party individual to your cause, but you do need to let them know that there is an issue at hand and you would like to resolve it with that person for the good of everyone involved. This ensures that no one involved in the situation, be it friend or family member, is caught off guard or thrown into the mix unnecessarily.

When you decide that the time has come to finally sit down and have a chat with that difficult individual, it is important to remain calm, collected, and open to what they are going to say as well. There are always two sides to every story, and if that person is difficult to you, you are probably just as difficult to them, so be aware of the fact that some of your flaws may be brought to light as well. Do not be combative or put your shields up if you begin to feel attacked, and in the event that the conversation becomes a bit more heated than it should be, you need to take action and put an end to it before things get worse.

Feel free to let the individual know that you are no longer comfortable with where the conversation is going and that you want to take a break until you both can calm down and regain your composure. If you need to have a third party "step in," there is nothing wrong with that, but make sure that person is someone who can mediate the situation without taking sides.

This can be tricky when it comes to dealing with family members. All too often you will find that there are not a lot of family members who are willing to step in and remain neutral. Most people do not want to get in the middle of things in case they are the target of the next issue, so more often than not, they will simply sit back and shut their mouths so they do not become involved one way or another, even if they are in total agreement with you.

If it becomes too much for you to handle and you can't find anyone to step in to assist in mediating the situation, there is another option, although there are very few people who want to take this step: family counseling. You may want to consider it if things are just too far out of control and you and the difficult person are just not able to resolve the situation on your own. While counseling is typically something that most people don't want to voluntarily sign up for, it can save your marriage or family in the long run.

Again, the most important thing you can do with regards to dealing with a difficult individual who is close to you is open the lines of communication; and if you can't do it alone or with a trusted family member or friend, you may need to seek the assistance of a licensed and trained professional in order to determine what course of action can assist you in bettering the relationship that exists between you and the person you are struggling with.

Unfortunately, sometimes it can become necessary to opt for not putting up with your difficult family member any longer, and there is nothing wrong with that either. If you have exhausted all other options, from trying to talk to them to seeking family counseling, you do have the option to cut ties with that difficult person for your own peace of mind and mental health. Depending on who the difficult person is, this option may make the holidays and family reunions a little hard to cope with, but sometimes a little distance and time apart can help to heal situations as well, on both sides.

As is the case when dealing with difficult individuals in the workplace, dealing with a difficult family member can be extremely hard to cope with. You see these individuals on a regular basis, and you want to make sure that things go smoothly and stress-free. Life is too short to deal with people who put you in difficult and stressful situations every time you see them. Be sure to speak up for your own sense of mental peace and well-being in order to ensure your own sanity, and also for the continued support and love within your family.

Chapter 4
Dealing with Difficult Parents

Difficult parental relationships are all too often the relationships that are the most challenging to interpret, understand, and heal from. From the earliest of ages we are taught to honor and respect our parents, to learn from them, and to trust them. And so many of us find ourselves putting our parents on pedestals that they simply do not deserve to be set upon.

In this chapter we will be shedding some light on what it means to have to deal with a difficult parent or parents. We will also be exploring the ideology of what it means to be a parent, why you do not have to be stuck in the all-consuming trap of being caught under the power of a difficult parent any longer, and how you can learn and grow from the experience as well.

It should first be said that no two parental relationships are the same. Just because a tip or a technique works well for one individual does not necessarily mean that it will work wonders for the next person who is struggling to deal with a difficult parent. That is precisely why it is of the utmost importance to understand that you need to reflect internally on the relationship that you have with your parents in order to better learn the proper reasoning techniques that may assist you in healing your relationship or simply making it a somewhat tolerable one at least.

When it comes to dealing with a difficult parental relationship, you need to do some self-reflection in order to uncover the reasons why your relationship is strained in the first place. Get out a piece of paper or a notebook or journal and take some time to answer some of the following questions so that you can better start to make sense of the relationship you have with your difficult parent or parents:

- When did you first notice that the issues were starting to arise? Have they always been difficult, from your earliest memory? Or did they become difficult later, such as in your teen years or early adulthood?
- Can you pinpoint any particular details that led to a change in their character? Divorce? Death in the family? Job loss?
- Have you tried talking to them about their difficult behavior? If yes, reflect on the conversation. If no, reflect on why you have not wanted to try.
- Is being difficult simply in their nature? Are their parents difficult as well?
- Are they only difficult at specific times? Family reunions? Holidays? Dinners or get-togethers with your family?

The more self-reflection you can put forth in terms of better attempting to understand your difficult parent or parents, the easier it will become to start to unlock the doors of their difficult behavior. By asking yourself certain questions, you will find that your mind will start to open up more and you can, in turn, start to pinpoint different things that may contribute to their behavior.

One thing should most certainly be noted: you can't change everyone, not even your parents, regardless of how much you may want to. Some people simply can't be changed, nor do they want to be changed. There is nothing wrong with that; you need to learn how to accept it and move forward with your own life, even if that means that you opt to no longer be around that person, or drastically limit your time with them, even if that person is your parent.

With that being said, you need to learn how to properly take the necessary steps to determine how you want to go about resolving the situation with your difficult parent. First things first, it's important to make sure that the lines of communication are open between you and your parent. If your parent is simply not open to discussing what is happening between the two of you and that their difficult traits are hindering your relationship, then you may need to give them some time for their own self-reflection as well.

A good way to do this is to plan a time where the two of you can sit down together to have a conversation. If possible, you may want to do this in public where people are a bit less likely to explode if they are feeling personally attacked. Sit down with your parent and approach them from a place of respect. No one likes to feel that they are being personally attacked, and this can easily occur when pointing out your parent's flaws and difficult characteristics, so you want to tread lightly.

Start the conversation out in a manner where they don't feel as if everything they have done is wrong. Try using neutral words such as "we" as opposed to "you," which can feel like a personal attack. Make statements such as "I feel ..." or "it feels like ... when ..." and share with them particular times when they were being difficult and how that affected you personally, or those around you personally. Again, tread lightly, pinpoint specifics, and be understanding with the fact that though they may be difficult, you are trying to address the situation before it gets out of control, and you are there for them and want to help them out before things get worse.

From here you'll know where you need to take the conversation, because it is most likely going to go one of two ways. The first way, and the most hopeful way, is that your difficult parent is going to hear you out and want to resolve the situation in order to mend the relationship with you. The second way is the complete opposite of that. They will end up putting up their defenses, getting angry, and either storm off or opt to change the subject.

Both of these situations are acceptable. Sure, the first way is ideal and what you are striving for and hope to achieve, and if that is the response you get, that's wonderful! You have a parent who is willing to work on bettering themselves in order to mend their overall relationship with you. That is more than most people get, and you are most certainly deserving of having that kind of bond with a parent, even a parent who can be difficult at times.

The second scenario, however, is one that is quite likely to occur, and you need to be well prepared for it to take place. Remind yourself that it is OK. You have opened the lines of communication with your difficult parent and taken the first steps in either repairing your relationship with your difficult parent or perhaps even having to walk away from them—temporarily or permanently—for your own sense of sanity and well-being.

After the initial conversation, you may want to take time to do some more self-reflection as to what your next course of action should be. Whether the conversation went well or whether it was an utter failure, you are going to need to determine where you should go from here. Be sure that you give your parent an ample amount of time to process the conversation and to reflect on what they have been doing, why they have been doing it, and who they have been harming in the process of being so difficult.

You can then plan on having a follow-up conversation with your parent so that the two of you can once again sit down and talk things out. You can choose the location of this second meeting depending on how the first one went. If it did not go as planned, you may want to meet in a public location to avoid an outburst, but if you feel that it went fine and you can continue the conversation in private, opt to have the private location somewhere you will both feel comfortable. For instance, if your parent is difficult because they do not get along with your spouse, you will want to avoid having such a conversation in your home with your spouse lingering in close proximity.

For the follow-up conversation, it is of the utmost importance that you once again stay calm, polite, and open to what they have to say as well. The conversation needs to flow with ease, and you both need to be allowed to speak openly about not only your parent's difficult traits but also some of the ways that you both feel they can be resolved, as well as where you both feel the triggers are stemming from. In this conversation, your parent will no longer be caught off guard with respect to the fact that they are being difficult, and they will now have the opportunity to improve by working on themselves and actively seeking out the proper options to do so, or they can simply continue ignoring that there is any issue at all.

This second conversation is going to be your best bet at determining where you need to go from here regarding how to handle the situation. If they are willing to work on themselves in order to break out of their difficult nature, this is wonderful news, and you need to be sure that you let them know you are there for them, that you support their desire to change, and that you are grateful they want to work on themselves in order to mend your relationship with each other.

If, on the contrary, they are still refusing to accept the fact that they are difficult and are not willing to change, you need to accept that fact and start considering what your next plan of action is going to be. Depending on what the issue is, you may need to take the action to distance yourself from your parent, either temporarily or permanently. Distance is one of the best ways to start the healing process. When you distance yourself from a difficult person, you are both able to reflect on the underlying issue at hand.

Creating distance between a parent, especially if you have been previously quite close with them, can be incredibly hard to do. All too often difficult people who refuse to accept that they are difficult do not see that they are doing or have been doing things that are creating tension between people around them, especially people that they love.

You can create distance a few different ways. The first way is to inform them that you need some space to sort through and process their reaction to your feelings about their behavior. While it is nice to give someone a heads up that you are going to give yourself some distance from them, sometimes they don't deserve that from you. If your difficult parent is acting harshly toward you or others that you care for, sometimes it is in your best interest and their best interest to cut ties without giving them a warning in advance.

When you cut ties without a heads up, you are sparking a sense of curiosity on your parent's part to wonder why you are distancing yourself in the first place. This shock of being "cut off" from your life gives them the chance to reflect on why you have severed ties with them, what they have done wrong, and the past conversations that you have had where you gave them the chance to assess their behavior and they opted not to.

Cutting ties with a difficult parent can be incredibly hard to do; however, as previously stated, it can all too often become necessary. Creating distance between one another provides both parties with a chance to do some inner reflection. While your parent is thinking about what they have done wrong, you can also reflect upon just how long you should keep those ties cut and if you even want to take the steps to attempt to mend the relationship. That thought may come as a shock to some people, but to others who have dealt with some painful situations associated with difficult parents, this may be just what is needed in order to heal themselves from the past.

Dealing with difficult parents can be incredibly hard to do. That is precisely why you need to ensure that you are taking all of the best steps to tread a bit lightly while also being direct about your feelings toward your actions. No one should make you feel as if you are not enough, or that those around you whom you care for are not enough, and if that is something that your difficult parent is doing, then you need to bring it up and make them aware they are doing it and how it is affecting you on a personal level.

If it becomes necessary for you to create some distance or even sever ties completely from your parent—whether temporarily or permanently—you need to be sure that you are ready for all of the repercussions that can also exist with this. You may end up getting hit with some backlash from other members of your family, and you may also end up not getting what you want from your difficult parent either. But you should also keep in mind that creating distance can be just what the doctor ordered in terms of healing your relationship with your parent as well. Creating distance can be hard to do, but it is often necessary; you need to determine what is in your best personal interest and if creating distance will be in any way beneficial to you, or both of you.

Just because your parent has given you life and raised you, it does not mean that they need to control you or make you or those around you feel bad about themselves or question how you are living your life, whom you choose to love, what career path you have chosen, or anything else. And again, you need to take care of yourself first and foremost. You can continue to love your parent and still opt to not be around them as much or even at all, until they have come to their senses and realized they have hurt you or those around you. Sometimes it takes drastic measures to spark drastic changes, and when it comes to dealing with difficult parents, this may be precisely what you need to do—especially if you have already attempted to talk to them multiple times about their actions and treatment and they are simply unwavering and unwilling to admit their faults and implement some change to better your relationship.

Do not be afraid to speak up to your parent to let them know how their actions are creating pain and harming those around them. You need to make sure that you are direct in your conversation, even if your words may be a bit hurtful to them, though you do not want to point fingers and put the blame on them in an unnecessarily harsh manner. Be clear, concise, honest, and direct so that they can see that you genuinely care about them and that you want to take the necessary steps to fix your relationship and build upon it. If they are just not ready to take those same steps, it is OK to walk away in order to give the both of you some time to reflect upon the situation and go from there. You may even want to offer up the suggestion that you and your parent get some professional family counseling in order to get the help you need to start the process of putting an end to their difficult behavior, and to kick-start repairing your relationship.

Again, and this cannot be repeated enough, it does not matter if it is a parent or not, you do not ever need to allow someone to make you feel awful or make your life miserable every time you are around them. Life is too short to find yourself being victimized or hurt by a difficult person, no matter who they are. The more open and honest you can be, not only with your parent but also with yourself, the easier it will be to process the relationship you have with your parent, and the easier it will be to try and mend the relationship as well. Keep the lines of communication open, always. Just because they potentially are not ready to work on themselves and fixing your relationship now, does not necessarily mean that they will not be ready to do so in the future. If you need to take a break from your parent or parents, there is most certainly nothing wrong with that, but you also need to make sure that you stay open enough to allow them to reenter your life.

When you give people the opportunity to come back into your life, you need to make sure that you are only permitting that reentry to fall under the specific terms that you set. It is perfectly acceptable to keep them a little at bay until you become more comfortable and accepting of their presence. When you set certain boundaries, you are showing them that you are in control of the situation in its entirety and that you can make the decision to ultimately distance yourself once again in the event that it proves necessary.

When you place boundaries and require people to abide by them, you are giving yourself the opportunity to control your circumstances and take back the power into your own hands. People need to respect you; you are deserving of it. And it should not matter who is causing your life to become difficult—even if it is a parent, you need to make sure that you take all of the proper measures and precautions to ensure your own happiness and that you have the capability to live your fullest and most happy life that you truly deserve.

Chapter 5
Dealing with Difficult In-Laws

Dealing with difficult in-laws is easily one of the hardest things to do for any married couple. It is also quite a popular struggle that many new couples have to deal with when getting together, getting engaged, and ultimately getting married. While for the most part in-laws will eventually come to accept their new son-in-law or daughter-in-law as being the one that their child has fallen in love with, sometimes parents just can't let go of the fact that they feel their son or daughter could have done better.

If you are struggling with issues related to in-laws, this chapter is for you. Here we will be evaluating why in-laws can be so hard to deal with and what steps you can take to begin the process of mending the relationship with them and building upon it from the ground up.

In-laws can be incredibly hard to deal with. Parents love their children, and all too often a good majority of parents have the feeling that there is no one who is good enough to be with their child. They place their children on a pedestal, and no one can support and care for their son or daughter as well as they can. While parents who love their kids in such an unwavering fashion are commendable and completely understandable, this most certainly puts a damper on things for the individual who is marrying their kid.

If you are recently engaged or married and having issues that pertain to your in-laws, you are not alone. There are so many people who have found themselves feeling like they are just not able to stand up to the in-law challenge, and who often feel as if they are not good enough to be married to the person simply because of how the in-laws treat them. And that just is not right, plain and simple. So what do you do about it?

Well, first and foremost, you need to talk to your significant other. Speaking to your significant other is going to be the best way to go about addressing the underlying issue at hand. When you speak to your significant other, you need to keep the lines of communication open, as is the case with bringing up issues related to difficult people and situations. Bringing up issues that pertain to their parents may very likely be a sensitive subject, particularly if they are close to them.

More than likely, however, your significant other will be well aware of the fact that their parents may be difficult in nature, or may be singling you out particularly because you are married to their son or daughter, but in no way should this justify or validate their behavior toward you.

Sit down with your significant other and calmly, but directly, tell them that you have concerns regarding the treatment of your in-laws toward you. Be open and honest about how you are feeling and where you believe it is stemming from, and offer some options that you think may end up helping you make the attempt to try and repair the difficult and strained relationship with your in-laws. You'll want to make sure that you tread lightly with regards to how you bring all of this up to your significant other, particularly if you are newly engaged or married and, as previously stated, they are close to their parents. Be sure that you invoke your significant other's opinion on the matter, ask for suggestions as to things you can do to discuss this difficult behavior with your in-laws, and ask your significant other to support you when the time comes to bring this issue up.

When you have the support of your significant other, it is a good time to proceed with arranging a sit-down meeting with your in-laws to bring some of these topics to light. You are going to want to make sure that you meet in a neutral location so everyone feels comfortable and up to having a conversation about such a difficult topic.

To kick-start the conversation, open with the fact that you love their son or daughter, and you have nothing but the utmost amount of respect for them as well, but you have some personal concerns regarding their treatment toward you. Keep the tone of the conversation polite in nature, but also a bit firm and to the point. You need to make sure that you are letting them know you are firm in your stance of not wanting to be treated that way any longer, and that their treatment toward you is completely unacceptable with respect to how in-laws should be treating their son-in-law or daughter-in-law. Do not come off as if you are attacking them, but stand firm in your statement, make sure that you bring up specific examples of when they were being difficult or downright nasty to you, and reiterate the fact that you love their son or daughter. You are in their life because of that love and you deserve to be treated with respect and dignity, regardless of their personal beliefs or misrepresentations about you.

One of the biggest things that you can address with your in-laws is to press the question of why they do not like you or why they feel the need to be difficult toward you in the first place. Bringing this up can be an important step in helping to assist in building up the relationship that you have with your in-laws. When you ask this, you are in actuality putting your in-laws on the spot in a manner that demands an answer. And if they can't answer the question, it gives them the opportunity to realize that they are, in fact, being difficult and that perhaps they need to change their attitude for the good of their son's or daughter's well-being, as well as yours, and their relationship with the both of you.

After you have made the initial confrontation with the parents of your significant other, you need to allow them the opportunity to process what specifically it is that you were trying to point out to them, and how they can take the proper action to begin the process of mending the relationship with both you and your significant other, while also determining why they felt the need to be difficult toward you in the first place. This break time after the initial conversation is the perfect opportunity for some self-reflection for all parties involved.

Dealing with issues related to difficult in-laws can be incredibly stressful for everyone. Your significant other will find that they are caught in the middle of the situation, and your in-laws may feel like they are being attacked or accused of something they simply were not aware they were doing in the first place. And you are the victim of the situation who is seeking some sort of resolution to the underlying issue at hand. This is by and large why dealing with difficult in-laws can be such an incredibly daunting task. You are going to need to take active steps to determine the proper course of action to proceed from here.

After the initial meeting, you'll want to arrange some sort of follow-up meeting in order to address the situation and figure out how everyone is feeling at this point, if there are any questions that need to be addressed, and if there are any issues that they personally want to bring up regarding you or your relationship with their son or daughter. This meeting may bring up some dirty laundry, but everything needs to be brought to the table in order to sort through it together, as a new family, and to figure out which issues are pressing and need to be resolved, and which ones are really quite petty and can be pushed to the side in order to keep moving forward.

When it comes to dealing with difficult in-laws, you should be honest with them. Again, you need to keep those lines of communication open in a clear and concise manner, while also maintaining the stance that you are firm and direct with regards to how you are feeling about their unnecessary treatment toward you. Ask questions about things like why they feel this way, why they feel compelled to have said this or done that, or how they feel you could improve upon certain things. The more questions you ask, the more the conversation will be properly directed to where it needs to be in order to find a desirable resolution.

Be sure to continuously keep your partner in the loop before, during, and after these meetings with your in-laws. Continue asking them questions as well about how they are feeling about the situation. Also ask if they are comfortable with regard to how everything is playing out and if they want to bring up any issues personally that pertain either to their parents, to you, or all of the above. Again, and I can't stress this enough, your partner is caught between a rock and a hard place when it comes to having to support you and addressing some potentially very uncomfortable issues with their parents. It is not a comfortable place to be, and it is going to be emotionally trying for them to go through. You want to make sure that you are continuously there for your significant other in order to ensure they are feeling OK with how the meetings are going, how you are handling the situation, and if they have any suggestions. You and your significant other are a team; you are going to need to stick together in order to create some welcome change with regards to dealing with your difficult in-laws.

After the second meeting, hopefully some of the ice will be broken and you and your in-laws will be able to proceed accordingly in favor of building a good, healthy relationship, or at least a tolerable one for the benefit of everyone involved.

Dealing with difficult in-laws can most certainly be an incredibly hard thing to do. Hopefully, you have in-laws that are willing to work on the relationship they have with you for the happiness and peace of mind of their son or daughter, because that should be the most important thing to them. If, however, you don't have in-laws who are willing to accept that you are going to be spending the rest of your life with their son or daughter, then you and your significant other will have to privately discuss how you both wish to address the situation in order to come up with a positive resolution.

It may become necessary for one or both of you to distance yourself from your in-laws. Whether this means stepping back from family dinners, brunches, or reunions, creating some distance can be precisely what you need to give yourself a much-needed break from them, while also providing them the opportunity to think about why you are no longer seeking to come around.

Regardless of whether your difficult in-laws are ready to take the steps to start working on their relationship with you or not, you are still going to need to take time to strengthen your relationship with your significant other in the meantime. The stronger your bond is with them, the easier it will be for the two of you to handle any situation that gets thrown your way. A strong bond with your significant other can get the two of you through anything.

Chapter 6
Dealing with Difficult Spouses

As is the case with dealing with difficult in-laws and parents, the issue of dealing with a difficult spouse is something that is incredibly hard to do. Your spouse is someone whom you have made the ultimate decision to spend the rest of your life with—through thick and thin. Unfortunately, one of the biggest issues that a lot of marriages end up being faced with is the issue of difficult spouses, who all too often will butt heads with their significant other. This is one of the reasons it is of the utmost importance to make sure that you have spent a significant amount of time with your significant other so that you can learn the ins and outs of their personality.

Even if your spouse ends up having a difficult personality or difficult traits, that should in no way take away from your relationship and desire to be successful in your relationship. There are a number of things that you can implement in order to find some middle ground for the both of you to be happy and to build upon your relationship in a manner that leads to as little difficulty as possible.

When it comes to dealing with a difficult spouse, you are most certainly going to have to tread a bit lightly. Regardless of how long the two of you have been together, you need to make sure that your relationship is kept open and honest. If there is some sort of problem, particularly with regards to dealing with issues that are related to difficult behavior traits, you need to make sure that you address the issues with an open and honest heart and mindset. Whether the issue has been going on quite a while now or their behavior is something that may have arisen from an issue that has recently affected them, you'll need to break the ice with them and bring it to their attention. More often than not, difficult people are not even aware of the fact that they are being difficult in the first place.

To break the ice, make them aware that you want to speak to them about something that has been bothering you, and ask when the time is right for the two of you to sit down and talk about the issue or their difficult behavior. It is important to not bring the issue up when you note that they are emotional about something, such as coming home from a stressful day of work, or are dealing with personal issues involving their family or other things. Find a time when your significant other is calm, collected, relaxed, and maybe in a good mood. Let them know that there is "nothing wrong," per se, but there has been something weighing on you and you just wanted to chat about it in order to better understand their feelings as well.

When you are ready to have the initial discussion with your significant other, make sure you make them feel comfortable and in no way, shape, or form suggest that they are personally being attacked or that their character is being attacked. Let them know that you have simply noticed a few things that have caused you concern with regard to them being portrayed as difficult, and you simply want to address why they have been acting that way in particular. You'll want to strive to bring up specific examples so that they can have a clear idea of what it is exactly that you are talking about. Be sure to inform them of when you first started to notice the difficult behavior, and ask if there is something they need from you that could assist them in coping with whatever it is they are personally dealing with that is leading them to be difficult in the first place.

People who are difficult in nature or who are simply dealing with something difficult for the time being can all too often be a bit emotional so, again, and I can't stress this enough, you are going to want to tread lightly so that your significant other does not in any way feel like they are being attacked or that they are doing something wrong that is causing you to be upset. Make sure they are well aware of the fact that you are on their team, that you want to know what is causing them to be difficult in the first place, and how you can be there for them and help them out with the situation they are dealing with.

Your significant other should feel the need to get close to you when you are bringing certain things to their attention, such as difficult behavior, and vice versa. This is specifically something that you should also bring to their attention during the discussion. Make sure that you let them know you are not accusing them of anything wrong, that you are most certainly not perfect either, and that you want to be there for them, in whatever way you can be that will help them out.

If at any time during the discussion you find that your their defenses are starting to go up and they are becoming angry or upset, you need to take the time to back off a bit and state that you are more than willing to take a break from the discussion and talk about it at a better time. Taking that stance is going to be the best way to prevent a huge outburst or argument that will end up getting the both of you nowhere beneficial and that will not be helpful in any way. It is OK to need to take a breather from an uncomfortable discussion, especially if it involves informing your significant other that they are being difficult. It is most definitely not a discussion that anyone wants to have with someone they love; however, it is so much better to bring these issues to light before they get significantly worse in the long run and lead to bigger issues in the future.

The second time you circle back to wanting to have this chat, you are going to approach your significant other in the same manner. Again, make sure that you inform them you are not trying to attack them in any way, but there are some issues that you are concerned with and want to address. Bring up a few different scenarios that you can think of where your partner was being difficult. Try not to pick a petty scenario where virtually anyone would have acted in a similar manner, but pick out a time where they have been really difficult and it was concerning to you so that they can get a clear idea of what you are talking about, why it is alarming to you, and why you want to discuss it further.

When you are able to bring certain examples up to your significant other that shed light as to why you are concerned about their behavior, then you can prove to them, in a sense, that there is an issue and it needs to be resolved for the benefit of your relationship. No one likes having to deal with difficult people; it can really weigh on one's mind, body, and soul, and no marriage or relationship should have to bear that added weight in addition to the multitude of other issues that couples are often faced with.

When you express your concerns over a spouse or partner's difficult behavior, you are taking matters into your own hands in order to resolve the underlying issue. The faster you are able to address the situation in order to find a proper resolution to it, the faster you can get your marriage or relationship back on track and pointed in the right direction.

Pointing out someone's difficult behavior can be incredibly hard to do. There is not a person alive who likes to hear about their imperfections or flawed characteristics. Your partner or spouse is most certainly going to be in that boat, and this is particularly true because you are the person that they love and trust the most in their life—and hearing you point out their poor behavior is undoubtedly not something that they are going to want to hear. That is precisely why you need to approach the situation with a bit of caution and tiptoe while still getting to the point. Reiterate the fact that you love and care for them, unconditionally, but that their difficult behavior is really weighing quite heavily on you and you want to know how you can help them deal with it and fix the underlying issue at hand.

When you are able to express that you love your spouse or partner and that you are going to stand by them, no matter what, they will be more willing to accept that perhaps they are, in fact, being a bit difficult and will want to come around to seeking the help they need either from you, or perhaps even a professional counselor—there is absolutely nothing wrong with that.

Difficult behavior can be incredibly hard to fix, especially by a person who fails to admit or see that there is even an issue in the first place. And if that is something you are noticing in your partner, you need to let them know that as well. Encourage them to see that while their behavior may be tough to deal with at times, you love them and you want to be there beside them to help them work on themselves in order to be the very best version of themselves.

If it comes down to your significant other needing a little bit more help than you are able to provide them with, there is again absolutely nothing wrong with seeking the assistance of a qualified professional counselor who can address the situation further and examine your partner's behavior a little more in depth in order to help them more effectively. There is most certainly no shame in needing more direct help, and you need to let your partner know that. Be sure to offer that you are willing to go with them to counseling so you can pick up some tips and techniques to help them cope with their emotions and manage them properly and effectively as they arise.

Having to deal with a partner or spouse who is difficult can be an insanely hard thing to do, but when you are ready and willing to speak to them about their behavior, and when they are actively ready to start working on modifying and correcting their behavior, then you will find that your relationship is capable of reaching an entirely new level of love and appreciation. Effective communication is something that many people have difficulty being able to accomplish, and if you are dealing with a difficult person who also not the best communicator regarding their thoughts, feelings, and emotions, you are going to have a tough time being able to break down that barrier.

That is precisely why it is incredibly important that you stay positive yet firm in your stance that they are being a bit difficult. It is crucial that you stay on top of their behavior and gently remind them they are being difficult, especially at a specific moment so they can see in real time what it is they are doing that is leading you to believe they are being so difficult in the first place.

Being married to a difficult person can be incredibly hard. I once spoke to a good friend of mine who had recently married his best friend. They had been together for about six years, had a child together, and finally decided that the time had come for the two of them to tie the knot. They figured since they had been together for so long and shared virtually every aspect of their lives together, there would be no surprises in the matrimonial bliss. Unfortunately, things and people change, particularly after getting married. While the couple had long been doing everything together for several years, including sharing bills, sharing a mortgage, and raising their child, things seemed to really take a turn once their last names were the same, and he could not figure out just why that was.

The strange thing about marriage is that two lives become one in an entirely different manner than when you are simply living together. Even with couples who have been together for a long time without being married, it is still a bit different. You start to get significantly more open and comfortable with one another, perhaps because you are in a "legal" relationship now, and that can really change people at times. I pointed this out to him and asked him what specifically was making her appear so different to him in terms of portraying difficult characteristics. His answer was an interesting one. Whenever he brought something to her attention, including issues that were related to her recent development of being incredibly difficult, she went into an instant shutdown mode and she refused to speak any further. She had never been this way before, and he was completely failing to understand why.

Their relationship had always seemed to be one where the two of them opted to get things out on the table, and now he could not even get her to answer questions about anything personal. How was work? Fine. What did you have for lunch? Salad. Did you see the artwork that Junior did at preschool? Yep. There was no communication, and he was beside himself with regards to trying to get her to open back up. He could not understand why the slightest push to get her to open up a little bit ended in a full-on blowout argument. They had only been officially married for seven months and yet he was already thinking that maybe a divorce would be inevitable.

I encouraged him that divorce was not the answer. There had to have been something that was plaguing her, and he needed to figure out what it was, by any means necessary. He spoke with her best friend, a coworker that they were mutual friends with, and finally her mother. And it was her mother who seemed to have the answer of what was affecting her daughter. She and her husband had recently told her that they were in the process of divorce themselves, and she was unable to get her feet stable enough to process this heavy blow that caused a whirlwind of emotions, so she shut down completely.

I informed him that he was going to need to approach bringing this up with the utmost sense of caution. No one likes to feel as if they have been "investigated," and he felt like that was what he had done. He ended up making arrangements to have a quiet dinner alone, just the two of them at a nice restaurant, to talk about the underlying issue that was afflicting his bride and causing such a drastic change in her personality. He was open and honest in saying that he was concerned about her, and in feeling this way, he reached out to the individuals that he had for a little insight. He was lucky because she was not angry. She understood why he had done what he had, and she apologized for keeping the divorce of her parents so hush-hush. She honestly did not know what to do, think, or feel, and she openly admitted that she had pushed him away, along with many others, so that she could process things on her own.

This is an interesting story to keep in mind, because you really can't judge a book by its cover. You never know what someone is dealing with, how they will handle it, and how their emotions will direct them to treating those around them in a different and often difficult manner. That can be true even with someone that you love and feel you know intimately. It is of the utmost importance to remember to stay positive and encouraging when it comes to dealing with a difficult spouse or partner. People handle their emotions differently, and sometimes it is OK to step back and allow them the opportunity to process whatever it is that they are dealing with, before really addressing your concerns. If you note that their behavior has quickly changed from being "normal" to difficult, or it seems that they are just not snapping out of their difficult traits, you should voice your concerns in a loving but direct manner. Be positive, loving, and encouraging, and make sure that you reiterate just how much you love them and are there for them, no matter what it is that you, your partner, or the both of you together have to go through.

    Love and marriage go through so many difficult things, but standing next to your significant other and ensuring them that you are in it through thick and thin, is going to save your relationship on so many levels. When it comes to a healthy marriage, you need to make sure that you always keep the lines of communication healthy, active, and efficient in order to really keep it effective. All too often, if you are with someone for an extended period of time, the two of you will feel as if you know each other so intimately that there is little left to be discussed and the "flame" of the relationship tends to burn out a little bit at a time.

    One of the best things that you and your partner can do is take the time to talk to each other, and not just about simple, everyday things like how your workday was. You both know all about that stuff and hear about it all the time—it is a well-worn conversation.

Keep things positive and upbeat by implementing fun ways to encourage your conversation to be a bit more exciting! Play twenty questions to really pull them out of the standard chats you tend to have each and every day, and engage your partner to come out of that shell they have built around themselves over the years. This is going to bring that spark back to your relationship in a manner that you both potentially have not experienced since you first got together.

The power of conversation truly is limitless, and the more you can bring your partner to that intimate level of engaging conversation, the more likely they will be to speak up to you whenever they are experiencing a personal problem, thus saving a ton of unnecessary disputes, arguments, and difficulties in the long run.

Chapter 7
Dealing with Difficult Children

Dealing with difficult children can be a bit of a tricky task because there are so many different things that affect children of different ages in varying manners. In this section we will be breaking down some of the main issues that make children difficult in order to specifically narrow down why they tend to act the way they do, and discuss how you can strategically work with your child to help them out.

When it comes to dealing with difficult children, you need to understand that the child is not being difficult intentionally or that there is not something necessarily wrong with them. Children, especially young children, have difficulties being able to process their emotions because they do not fully understand them. It is of the utmost importance that anyone who deals with children, whether their own or the children of others, understands how to successfully navigate the feelings and emotions of a difficult child. This is crucial in order to ensure that the child will end up thriving emotionally, and that you will have the greatest possible relationship with the child so that they feel as accepted, loved, and connected as possible.

When you have to deal with a difficult child, it is perfectly normal to feel frustrated, sad, and upset. Difficult children can be extremely challenging, and if you resist or deny that you are feeling these emotions, you can't be there for your child with a clear head. Keep in mind that this kind of behavior in children is something they usually will grow out of if intervention is taken in the form of creating boundaries and a nurturing environment. Children do not purposely misbehave; their developmental drive to explore and experiment is significantly stronger than their impulse to act, their ability to control themselves, and their ability to regulate their behavior. You really need to take that into consideration when you are dealing with a difficult child.

Some of the best tips to help your child readjust their difficult behavior are as follows:

- **Trust yourself.** You need to make sure that you do what feels right for you, the child, and the situation at hand. You know how to handle these difficult situations, and you need to trust your gut instinct in order to successfully handle each situation as it arises.
- **Be consistent.** Consistency is incredibly important, and you need to make sure that you do not give up. Once you have decided to do something, you need to set your mind to doing it. Regardless of what plan you have set in place for your child, you need to stick with it. Children thrive on consistency; the more consistent you can be with regards to setting a schedule for them or implementing certain ideas about how to readjust their difficult behavior, the better. You need to make sure that you stay with the plan no matter what.
- **Do not overreact.** This can be hard to accomplish when you are feeling a little overwhelmed about the child's behavior; however, it is vital that you do not overreact to how they are dealing with their emotions. Allow the child to work through whatever it is that they are dealing with and simply be there for them when they are ready to come to you.

- **Talk to the child.** If the child is old enough, make sure that you talk to them about their behavior and how they are handling their emotions. When you are able to teach your child about their emotions, you are teaching them how to regulate their emotions as well. And this is one of the best ways to get them to practice better behavior in the long run and for them to learn how to control their emotions so they do not build up and lead to difficult behavior.
- **Be positive.** As difficult as it may seem, especially when you are in the midst of dealing with a child's tantrum, you need to try and stay as positive and encouraging as possible. If you get upset, you are teaching the child that they should follow suit and do the same thing, and this ends up becoming a vicious cycle. The more positive you can be, the more you are going to show the child that they should mimic your behavior. Instead of acting out and lashing out, the child will, in turn, learn how to properly regulate their emotions and control them in a proper manner.
- **Implement a reward system.** Implementing a reward system is a great way to encourage the child to change their behavior for the better. Sticker charts are good options for younger children because the child can see visually where they are in reaching their goal to earn a reward. If you are dealing with an older child, however, you may just want to discuss the terms and details of what they can potentially be rewarded with if they work on their difficult behavior and they start to show signs of improvement.

Depending on the age of the child, you need to learn how to adapt to the difficult behavior they are exhibiting and effectively take the proper measures to teach them the tools they need in order to correct that behavior. Dealing with a difficult child is hard to do. You care for the child deeply and you want to help them learn how to work through their emotions, but it can be quite hard to accomplish. Especially if you are dealing with a young child who does not understand or know how to properly process and handle their emotions and what they are internally experiencing.

If you have tried to assist the child in changing their difficult behavior to no avail, you may need to seek the help of a professional counselor, child psychologist, or child behavioral therapist in order to determine if there may be an underlying condition that should be examined.

There are a number of issues that children deal with where they do not understand what is happening to them or why they are feeling a certain way, and because they can't properly process their emotions and what is going on, they will start to act out in ways that make them appear difficult. In reality they are simply struggling and do not know what else to do.

If you are making note of the fact that your child is dealing with issues that you just can't help them with, you may want to go about meeting with a professional in order to find some help and some answers. Here are some red flags that indicate you may need to consider seeking the help of a professional:

- Behavior problems at daycare, school, or in the home or your community that are ongoing.
- Temper tantrums that are unexplainable and occur frequently.

- The inability to sit still, constant movement that's not associated with normal play, or hyperactive behavior.
- Not wanting to participate or having difficulties participating in normal activities for your child's age range.
- Unusual or strange worries and fears.
- Problems with organization, concentration, and attention span.
- Getting stuck, so to speak, on a certain action, activity, or thought that they can't get past.
- Withdrawing from activities they used to enjoy doing or friends they used to enjoy spending time with.
- Unusual or strange beliefs, behavior, or feelings that are out of character for them.
- A lack of energy, even when rested, that is ongoing.
- Difficulty waking up, going to sleep, or staying asleep.
- Sudden, explosive emotional outbursts or similar reactions.
- Prolonged negative attitude or moods.
- Frequent complaints for no apparent reason.
- Inability to deal with problems that arise.
- Feelings of sadness or hopelessness without a reason that don't go away.
- Wanting to be alone all or most of the time.
- Inappropriate or unusual reactions toward adults or children.
- Persistent nightmares or night terrors.
- Visions, delusions, or hearing things that are not real.
- Significant changes in their behavior over a short duration of time.
- Problems with eating, such as eating too little or too much.

- Refusal or just not wanting to go to school on a consistent basis and a noticeable decline in their performance at school, which is usually because they refuse to do their schoolwork.
- Violence toward themselves, other people, property, or animals.
- Deliberate aggression or disobedience.
- Little to no remorse for not following the rules and a deliberate refusal to listen to authority figures.
- Self-harm or self-injury.
- Volatile mood swings.
- The inability or unwillingness to make their own decisions.
- Speaking so rapidly that they are difficult to understand or interrupt.
- Unable to get along with others in most situations.
- Constant worrying about virtually everything, even minor issues, on a consistent basis.
- Becoming easily angered or bored or displaying other overly emotional behavior along with the inability to cope with their problems.

Please take note of the fact that this list is not even close to being exclusive. And it should be noted that often some of the symptoms that are listed can be the result of significant changes in the life of the child, such as a death or divorce in their family, illness, a change of school, moving to a new area, or a new sibling. However, sometimes the aforementioned things can arise and have no apparent reason at all.

It is completely understandable that it can be quite difficult to be 100% sure that the child is going to require some help, and more often than not it is even harder to accept the fact that the child may potentially have some sort of mental, emotional, or behavioral health-related issue. It is these same thoughts that can easily prevent us from seeking out the assistance that our children are in need of. One of the most important things that you need to keep in mind is that the mental health of your child is treatable. And when children are properly connected to the right care and treatment, you will find that they are supported and they, in turn, can go on to live happier and more successful lives as you continue to manage their symptoms of mental health.

When it comes to parenting or otherwise playing a role in the life of a "difficult" child, you need to make sure that you trust your instincts, and you need to be open to seeking help if you truly believe that the child may require it. Your natural gut instinct will never lead you astray, and it is incredibly important to make sure that you follow it, especially in the interest of the overall well-being of a child. Pay close attention to the child; if something doesn't seem right, it more than likely is not, and the earliest possible intervention can do wonders in the long run.

Communication is very important when it comes to dealing with a child who is acting difficult. Make sure they are aware of the fact that it is OK to release their emotions, but they need to understand that there is a proper way to do so. Lashing out negatively or harming those around them is most certainly not the way to go about handling things. Let the child know that you are there for them, and if they need to talk about their emotions, you will be there to listen and help them out in any way that you can. When a child feels that they can trust you, they will be significantly more likely to turn to you when they are having a problem and do not know where else to go.

When your child is going through something, it is important to determine what the underlying issue is that is causing them to react the way they are. Ask your child to try and describe how or what they are feeling so that you can, in turn, get a better idea of what they are experiencing as a whole. Just because they can't tell you the specific name of what they are struggling with does not mean that they are not able to describe the emotion, when it started, and when it gets going inside of them. When you have a better understanding of their struggle, you can better begin the process of helping them on the level that they really need.

It can be very hard to get a child to break out of their shell when they are struggling with certain issues that they can't explain. Make sure that you take the time to be with your child. If he or she wants to be alone, it is OK to give them their space, but do not leave them unattended for extended durations, which can lead to much larger issues in the long run of their development. They can end up developing issues that are related to abandonment, anxiety, and depression. If your child wants to be left alone, accept that, but make sure that you pop in their room to check on them and let them know that they are loved. Also let them know that while you are there for them, you will respect their space until they are ready to talk.

When it comes to dealing with difficult children, patience is the key to assisting your child. You need to make sure that you change your perspective in order to ensure that you do not get angry with your child, and that you can recognize they are simply being difficult and the issue will pass. It is totally normal to feel angry, stressed-out, upset, or irritated; however, your child does not deserve to have you at your worst. When they see you in such a manner it can cause a whirlwind of confusing emotions that will only lead to your child's difficult behavior potentially getting even worse. And that is the very last thing that you need or want. The more you can keep calm and keep your composure, the easier it will be to figure out what your next plan of action should be in terms of dealing with your child's difficult behavior.

The better your own mental state is, the easier it will be to make sure that you stay very patient when dealing with a difficult child. You need to make sure you take care of your own mental health in order to stay calm, collected, and prepared to handle even the most difficult times. If your mental health is wearing down, you need to figure out a way to take some time for yourself. We will be discussing this a little more in depth in one of the following chapters, but please note that you need to really have your A game in place when it comes to dealing with a difficult child. They deserve the best versions of us, and if you are finding that you are not the best possible version of yourself, you need to make sure that you develop a course of action that can put you back into a good mental place so you can properly be there to love and support your child.

Try to stay positive and encourage your child to change their behavior by reminding them that they are acting inappropriately and that it is time to bring themselves back around to act properly. Be honest with your child, remind them that they know how to act properly, and tell them when their behavior needs to improve. If you are finding that your child is not listening to you at all, you should warn them that if their behavior does not improve, you will have to discipline them in order to correct their behavior. And if that still is not effective, you need to follow through with the disciplinary measures in order to properly modify their behavior and get them to think about what they are doing, what they have done wrong, and how they can do better in the future. When the punishment is complete, make sure you sit your child down and ask them to reflect on what just took place, how they felt about it, and what they can do to change their behavior in order to ensure that it does not happen again.

The big takeaway here is that you need to remain consistent when it comes to dealing with a difficult child. Children thrive on schedules and on consistency, and if you are not consistent in assisting your difficult child in learning how to act properly and modifying their behavior when it is just not right, then your child will remain difficult. In fact, the child will more than likely get even worse because they think acting in that manner is OK when there are no consequences that it will result in. When your child acts improperly, regardless of where you are, you need to make sure that you discipline them. If you are sitting in a restaurant and your child starts throwing a temper tantrum, they need to be removed from the restaurant and the situation needs to be handled immediately instead of waiting until you get back home.

It can be hard to discipline your child. I have seen so many parents try to put their child in time-out, but they end up feeling guilty about it and letting the child out of time-out before they serve the amount of time that they were told they needed to.

Stick with the punishment and do not cave in. If you end up caving in, your child will end up walking all over you because they believe that they can. This is a very important thing to keep in mind because once the teenage years start, you will have a ruthless kid who does whatever they want, whenever they want, and there is nothing that you can do about it. And that is an incredibly dangerous thing when you are dealing with young people who are trying to see what they can get away with.

Chapter 8
Dealing with Difficult Teens

Dealing with a difficult teen requires a chapter all its own, largely because their emotions are so different from that of a child's and an adult's. Teens are struggling to find out who they are, their place in this world, and how to be in control of any type of situations that arise. However, they all too often find themselves in a place where their emotions are running rampant, and they don't know how to properly process just what it is that is going on in their heads. In this chapter, we will be exploring the minds of teenagers so that we can better come to understand why they are being so difficult in the first place, and what exactly it is that we can do to help them cope instead of lash out.

First things first, you need to take into consideration how you were as a teenager. Sit down and think a bit about the things that you went through, the thoughts that you had, and the emotions that you experienced. The more that you can put yourself into the shoes of the teenager, the easier it will be to meet with them on their level and convince them that they can trust you so they can open up if they want or need to. You need to make sure you are extra patient with teenagers because—I am quite sure you are already aware of this—they tend to be quite moody and are quick to put their defenses up and become combative about their emotions. Make sure that if you recognize that your teen is dealing with something personal, you let them know that you are concerned about them. Then be comfortable just leaving it at that for the time being. If you see that their difficult behavior begins to subside, congratulations. If, however, their difficult behavior does not go away, you may need to come up with some sort of intervention plan to determine what is leading them to be so difficult and how you can help them. Here are some things that you can try in order to help your teen get through their issue in the best possible way:

Do not give them your power. A very common characteristic of a difficult teenager is that they seem to get a kick out of pushing your buttons, which triggers you and causes you to react negatively. Certain things such as breaking the rules, throwing a tantrum, teasing you, disobeying you, talking back, not listening to you, dismissing you, and provoking you are all little tactics that can trigger you to react in a manner that is simply not productive for either of you.

The more upset and reactive you act toward how they are acting, the more power you are giving your teen. You need to be sure that you keep your cool when you are dealing with a difficult teen. The less you react to the situation at hand, the easier it will be for you to handle the situation effectively with a clear and concise manner of thinking.

When you start to feel angry or challenged by your teen, try to avoid saying things that are going to make the situation worse. Step back, take a deep breath, and slowly count to ten. Often by the time you get to ten, you will have likely regained your composure and potentially found a better way to respond to the issue. This way you can reduce the problem as opposed to elevating it. If you are still upset over the issue after counting to ten, walk away from the problem and come back to it once you have had some time to calm down and think about things a bit.

Have set boundaries. Teens strive to attain their selfhood and independence, and that is why they opt to challenge authority—they want to see just how much power they have. Setting boundaries enables you to maintain a constructive and workable relationship with your teen. Boundaries must be laid out in a clear and concise manner, and you need to make sure that you hold your teen accountable to them.

The most effective boundaries are reasonable, fair, and consistently applied. If your teen has been acting difficult for some time, you need to communicate the boundaries that you are implementing and let them know that from here on out, they will be expected to abide by them or there will be consequences.

The first boundary you need to set is that your teen must treat you and others with respect. If your teen shows respect toward you, you can then grant them certain privileges based on the situation as you see fit. In terms of the other boundaries you set, those are up to you as they may be related to the family, their schooling, etc. Keep your list of boundaries relatively short but also clear, concise, and in writing.

Use effective and assertive communication. When you are dealing with a difficult teenager you need to make sure that you are strengthening your position of authority by using communication skills that are both effective and assertive. It is more than OK to put your foot down and tell your teen "no" when it is necessary. You need to demand respect from them, and you will not get that if your communication skills are simply invalid to your teenager and they simply do not care.

Use humor and empathy. If the situation at hand is relatively mild, show your teen some empathy by trying not to overreact. Respond to your teen by smiling instead of frowning, remind yourself that your teenager is simply being difficult yet again, and keep going about what you were doing. Try not to tell them what they should do if their issue is trivial.

Unsolicited persistent advice is annoying to your teen, and it may be perceived as a threat to their individualism and their selfhood. When your teen gets upset with you, instead of feeling anxious, irritated, and angry, give yourself a little bit of space, take a few breaths, and say to your teen, "This must not be easy." It is important to keep in mind that being empathetic does not excuse their unacceptable behavior.

When it comes to showing empathy to your teen, you need to keep reminding yourself that the vast majority of teens are struggling on the inside, and that being mindful of their personal experience can assist you in being able to relate to them with a sense of detachment yet understanding.

Let them find a solution. Difficult teenagers behave in the ways that they do because they truly believe adults do not listen to them or care how they are feeling. When you see that your teen is upset, offer up the option to talk to you. Say something along the lines of "I'm here for you if you want to talk." Make yourself available to chat, and remind them of that periodically, but do not be persistent or insist on trying to get them to open up if they do not want to or are just not ready to.

When you are communicating with your teen about what they are experiencing, listen but do not comment for a while. Be there as a "friend" of sorts and allow them to feel comfortable disclosing information with you. Before offering any input, ask them if they want to hear your advice. You may opt to say something along the lines of "Do you want to know what I think? If not, that is totally OK, I am here to listen." When you use effective communication, you are showing your teen that you are going to listen and support them and are also available for advice, even if they are unwilling to hear it.

Another smart tactic you may want to implement is that when you are dealing with some of your own personal issues, ask the teen to join you when you are trying to figure out a solution. Ask their input on what they would do and how they would handle the issue to see if they can come up with some constructive ideas. Try to avoid finding one single course of action; instead, evaluate multiple options with your teen's input as well so that the two of you can try to figure out a reasonable arrangement to handle your situation.

Deploy consequences. When your teen violates the rules, regulations, and boundaries that you set in motion and will not abide by them, you are going to need to start to deploy proper consequences. When you are able to properly identify the issue and are capable of asserting the right consequences, it is easily one of the most powerfully effective tools that we can utilize in order to make a difficult person, particularly a difficult teen, stand down. Consequences must be effectively articulated in order to make the teen pause regarding the situation at hand and think about their actions, even if just for a minute, and it will hopefully compel them to make a proper shift that takes them from resisting to cooperating.

It is important to keep in mind that more often than not your teen's difficult behavior is not deliberate. In fact, your teenager has very little control over their difficult attitude. Teens do not tend to manipulate you on purpose—it is not like they do nothing more than spend time in their room devising a scheme over new and improved ways to dig at you. To the contrary, your teen is a victim as well. Teens are faced with so many different pressing issues, from biological to psychological; they are experiencing so many changes during these years; and they have little to no control over them. They are dealing with a rollercoaster ride of emotions, and you are on the ride with them as well.

The brain changes that a teen experiences are quite extensive. In addition, there is significantly more rapid development within the brain functions and different areas that greatly increase impulsivity and risk-taking, and this is largely why they are so likely to be influenced by their peers. The areas of their brain function and structure that we can only wish would quickly become more well established during the teen years, like rational decision-making, self-control, and restraint, come along quite slowly during these years and do not fully develop until a bit later in their adolescence. Teens experience all of these various changes quite differently; however, it is crucial that parents know that teens realistically can't turn their emotions on or off simply based upon the things we do or say. And you need to exhibit a bit of patience and understanding with whatever it is they are going through.

Something that you need to keep in mind, however, is that you should closely watch your teen during these tumultuous years. While their difficult emotions tend to come and go, if you make note of the fact that their emotions are no longer "going," it may come down to the point where you need to seek professional help for your teen in order to make sure the emotions that they are experiencing are in fact normal; they could be the result of an underlying issue that they simply are not able to shake. While the vast majority of the difficult issues

that your teen is experiencing are completely normal, you should be on the lookout for the following red flags:
- Sleeping excessively or changes in their sleep pattern (beyond normal insomnia or general fatigue).
- Sudden changes in their academic performance (usually for the worse, but for the better can often indicate prescription abuse).
- Difficulty concentrating.
- Drastic changes in their eating habits (this can often be a red flag for an eating disorder).
- Unexplained weight loss or weight gain.
- Issues related to body image.
- Complete loss of overall interest in normal activities as well as the things they used to enjoy doing.
- Isolation (both at home and in school).
- Drastic changes in their personality (becoming angrier, more withdrawn, more aggressive, excessive moodiness, irritability, crying a lot, etc.).
- Feelings of helplessness or worthlessness.
- Being overly sensitive to normal criticism.
- Suicidal thoughts or actions or self-mutilation (such as cutting).
- Unexplained aches and pains.
- Keeping secrets from you and those around you.

Teens have this innate thing about them where they think that their parents don't understand what they are going through, so they hide themselves away and push people away as well, thinking that they can do everything on their own and handle things themselves. This is where you need to make sure that you are watching your teen's behavior and noting any significant and drastic changes that start taking place. Reach out to your teen, making sure that you always keep your conversations free of judgement, criticism, or condemnation.

The last thing you want to do is push your teenager even further away, and acting in such a manner will most certainly make that happen. Let your teenager know that you understand what they are going through; maybe even bring up some similar issues that you went through when you were a teen as well so they can truly see that you really do get it and are not just saying it. Again, remember what it was like when you were a teenager and all of the things that you personally felt, experienced, and went through. Get down to their level and open that line of communication so that they feel they can trust you and open up to you about what they are dealing with.

I wanted to take the time to share with you one example of a good friend of mine who recently went through a hard time with her teenage daughter. We'll go over some of the red flags that she ended up noticing and the actions that she subsequently took to save her daughter's life and build their relationship as well.

The issue started when her daughter was about fourteen years of age. Her daughter's behavior did a 180, and she was not sure just what the underlying cause behind the issue could be. She had made multiple attempts to ask her daughter what was bothering her, if there was anything that she could do to help, and when it had started, but the questions fell on deaf ears. Her daughter ended up shutting down and shutting her out completely.

When her daughter was not shut in her room ignoring the family, she had nothing but rude or condescending remarks for everyone she came in contact with. She used to be such a good, sweet girl, and now it seemed to her mother that she was losing her little girl.

She had also made note of the fact that her daughter's image was starting to change. She was eating tremendously less than normal, not sleeping well at night, and always wearing long sleeves, even on the hottest of summer days. Her mother was worried, but she was also completely unaware as to how she should work through the problem and help her daughter in sorting out her issues. Talking was not working, disciplinary action was not working, and empathy was not working, so she found herself at a complete loss as to which direction to go. She found herself considering therapy, but she was a bit concerned as to whether it would actually work or if it would be a waste of time and only drive her daughter further away.

Before she opted to book an actual appointment with a professional therapist, she wanted to try something first. She asked her daughter to go for a drive with her. Initially she was met with an unsurprising eye roll, but she really had no other option, so she climbed in the car.

My friend said that the whole drive her daughter was silent and that her words were ignored again, but she kept talking anyway. The two of them ended up parked in a pretty desolate area that has very little traffic but an exceptional view. My friend started the conversation by stating that she was concerned about what was going on with her daughter, she needed to know what the issue was, and she was at the end of her rope regarding her daughter's behavior. Again, silence, so she pressed on and gave her daughter an ultimatum: she could spill the beans about how she was acting and what it was that was behind her actions, she could go into a teen-help facility, or she could start meeting regularly with a professional. Again, silence, but not for long.

Her daughter admitted that she was being bullied at school and she had started to have thoughts about suicide. She said that she was afraid of being successful at taking her own life, so she had turned to cutting herself in order to allow her to control the internal pain by creating pain on the outside of her body. She was also severely struggling with her body image due to the bullying and had turned to bulimia (eating very little and then expelling it from the body).

My friend was right. She was losing her baby girl, but she was also at a point where she did not know what steps to take next. Her daughter was in tears as she broke down and expressed all of these issues that she was facing, and my friend found herself questioning if she was the one to blame. Had she paid enough attention to her daughter over the years? Had she missed the red flags that were placed in front of her? Had she provided enough love? Where had she gone wrong in her parenting?

The question really boils down to if she was even at fault at all, and the answer was that no one was really at fault. My friend was a remarkable mother who was always there for her daughter and always had been over the years. Her daughter, however, was just dealing with many emotions that she was unable to process on her own. Teens have a tremendous amount of difficulty dealing with their emotions on their own, and when you add in the things thrown at them daily, such as raging hormones, mixed and confusing emotions, and, in the case of my friend's daughter, bullying, you have a wild mixture of issues that are hard to cope with.

My friend had taken the proper measures to confront her daughter in a manner that worked in the best interest of both of them. Her daughter was not providing any solid answers, so she gave her an ultimatum: fess up or go to treatment. She fessed up. This conversation eventually led to them finding a different level of mutual understanding, and it really opened the lines of communication between them, which changed the entire course of their future relationship.

In addition to the self-mutilation and eating disorders, it turned out that her daughter was also drinking quite heavily, so the two of them agreed that seeking professional help would be in her best interest. She did not want to go to a teen treatment center, so she opted to seek out the help of a professional therapist. In the event that things could not be resolved in that manner, they would be forced to find a treatment center in order to make sure that she was receiving the help and support that she really needed.

The aforementioned scenario is one that is unfortunately all too familiar for parents of teenagers, and it can prove to be one of the most difficult times that parents have to endure in their roles of parenting. The main thing that you need to keep in mind is that your teenager is not the same person they were when they were smaller. They are constantly growing, changing, developing, and evolving over the course of their teenage years, and you need to be sure you remember that as your child ages and grows up. They are never going to be the same person that they were when they were younger, but if you can meet your teen where they stand and show them the ropes, then they can develop into the best possible version of themselves, which is a remarkable thing for any parent to experience.

It can be said that we only want what is best for our children, and when you are dealing with a teenager, that is most definitely not something that they are going to believe. All too often you will find yourself face-to-face with a combative teen who thinks that you are the enemy, that you are controlling them into what you deem is right, and that their opinion doesn't matter. You need to be sure that you show your teen that their belief system and the things that they want to achieve are valid, and while there are undoubtedly going to be circumstances where they make mistakes, you are going to be there for them no matter what. Even if the mistake leads to consequences, you are still in your teen's corner regardless of the situation at hand.

Difficult situations are a great opportunity for the both of you to learn and grow. Even though the situations can be a little bit of a daunting task that may seem impossible to get through at the time, the more open and honest you are with your teen, the easier it will be to handle each situation as it arises. Each and every time the two of you go through a difficult ordeal, you learn from the situation and can end up growing from it. When the two of you are successful at working through an issue, or even if you fail, you will still be able to take something away from the situation and learn what to do, or what not to do, next time.

Something else that you should consider is that not every interaction with your teen is going to be a negative one, and you need to remember that when the good times come, you should embrace them. Enjoy those good times with your teen—the smiles, the laughs, the jokes, and even the smart-ass comments.

As previously stated, your teen is going through a lot, so when they break out of their isolation and emotions, and you catch that ray of light beaming within them, you can take the time to really enjoy your teenager, even if for only a small bit of time. And be sure to commend them on their positive behavior. Give them a smile or nod of approval and tell them that it is good to see them smile, or that you really needed a laugh and appreciate their jokes. Little things like that are going to bring your teenager back around to make them feel appreciated and like their voice, their personality, and their presence genuinely matter to you.

Though those happy times may seem like they are few and far between, enjoy them when they happen. However, if it comes down to the fact that you need to dish out punishment to your teen, you should be as mild as you can be depending on what it is that they have done. Late for curfew? They will not be going out the following weekend. Failed a test? Less electronic use for them.

When you are capable of dishing out mild punishment, you are making sure your teen will not want to have to deal with the punishment again and will think twice about their actions next time. However, if the punishment is too lenient, they are more apt to take advantage of you and the situation, knowing that whatever punishment they received last time was not that bad. On the other hand, if the punishment you hand out to them is too harsh, they are going to go into that angry shutdown mode, and you will be faced with one pissed off teen who may seek to get back at you by acting even worse.

Make sure you keep your punishment somewhere in the middle of the road. If they continue acting out after receiving mild punishment, then you may need to upgrade your punishment a little at a time in order to find that middle ground so that your teen can learn from their mistakes and grow from them as well.

When it comes to raising teens, you also need to make sure that you find time to compromise a little as well. Teenagers all too often feel as if they have virtually no control of their situation, and when it comes to allowing them freedom you need to be willing to make some compromises in regards to what you allow them to do. If they want to go out and do something, be willing to work with that, but make sure that you lay down some ground rules as well as far as what they can and can't do, and what they should and shouldn't do. Be flexible about the clothing they choose to wear or the hairstyle or hair color they want to try out, and allow your teen to have the opportunity to be able to find and express themselves.

Similar to the case of dishing out a harsh punishment, when you opt to not compromise a little and give your teen some freedom to express themselves and do their own thing, they are going to push back and try to fight for their freedom. This can ultimately lead to much larger problems in the long run. Be willing to work with your teenager instead of against them so that the two of you can end up building a stronger relationship that is built on a sense of mutual trust and appreciation.

The more you blatantly refuse to allow your teen to do something, the more they are going to want to do it, and they will take basically any action necessary to make sure they are successful in accomplishing whatever it is. The more you can compromise, the easier you can make things happen in your favor, which can save you many unnecessary battles with your teen. They will go on to believe they can come to you and ask for certain things and may actually have some success in getting what they want because you are showing them that you trust them.

Realistically, when it comes down to it, you know what is best for your teenager. You know them inside and out and have been alongside them for the roller-coaster ride that is parenting for many years now. You also know what methods work and which ones don't work for your teenager. However, the aforementioned tips are there to give you a couple of different options to work with in order to see if perhaps one may end up working for your personal needs as well as for your teen.

    Be sure to try and keep an open mind when issues arise, remind yourself again of how you were at that age, take a few breaths, and push through to determine what the best option is going to be for yourself and your teenager. The more open-minded and patient you can be, the easier it will be to proceed with handling challenging issues with a better train of thought overall, and that can be incredibly beneficial to both you and your teen and lead to a much stronger bond between you both as well.

Chapter 9
Dealing with Difficult People as a Whole

In this chapter, we will be tackling the issue of coming in contact with difficult people and what strategies in particular you can use to deal with them. Whether the person is a waiter or waitress, a DMV employee, or simply someone cutting you off in traffic, we all have to come in contact with difficult people at some point. The hardest thing about dealing with difficult people as a whole is that you don't know them personally, so it can be hard to determine how you need to handle the situation. Do you smile and let it pass? Do you say something? Here we will be exploring some of the best ways that you can deal with the difficult people you may randomly encounter on a daily basis.

To get started, it is of the utmost importance to understand that difficult people are everywhere, and you are bound to come into contact with them at any given time throughout your day, week, or month. This is especially the case if you work in a place where dealing with difficult people is basically inevitable—customer service in particular is one of the best examples. And learning how to properly safeguard your mental state is one of the best ways to go about dealing with these types of people.

I once knew an individual who worked in customer service for a moving company that was based in Brooklyn, New York. She liked the job well enough and got along with all of her coworkers and the individuals in management, but she was an incredibly sweet person who lacked the ability to process the many customers who called each and every day demanding to know why their movers were late, why something was broken or lost in the process of transit, or why the move would cost so much. It was a surprisingly cutthroat job that she admitted she didn't believe she was cut out for.

Customer service is a brutal position, and most people who don't work in it cannot understand just how emotionally demanding the position is in terms of having to deal with angry people, stressed-out people, and difficult people every day. It can be quite daunting, to say the very least. Unfortunately, she ended up leaving the position for something she was a bit more suited to handle on an emotional level, and while she is happy at her new job, we ended up chatting the other day about her regrets that she could not "buck up" and just do the customer service job.

The thing about dealing with difficult people, I explained to her, is that when you are hit by them over and over and over again, it's hard to just let them keep knocking you down. Ultimately, you throw your hands up in the air and admit that maybe you just are not cut out to deal with them. There is nothing wrong with that. The vast majority of people out there do not want to deal with angry, stressed-out, or difficult people. That is a fact of human nature. Not everyone is cut out to do it, and some people are just better at handling certain situations than others. Again, there is nothing wrong with that, but you need to be aware of the fact that before you decide to quit your job and pack your things to leave, there are some effective strategies that we will cover in this chapter.

I first want to bring up the fact that in any situation when you are dealing with difficult individuals you don't know, you need to tread lightly with regards to the situation at hand.

I say this only because we live in some pretty crazy times. There are countless stories of road rage incidents, shootings at office buildings and stores by disgruntled customers—the list goes on and on. You never truly know whom you are dealing with, which is why you need to tread lightly and not overreact to the situation.

If you are dealing with an irate customer, listen to what they have to say, be polite, and inform them that you will handle the situation. If they refuse to be talked down from the ledge, inform them that you will get a supervisor to assist them immediately and pull yourself away from the situation. Be polite, but do not be a victim or a target of their lashing out. If the irate person is someone who just cut you off in traffic, smile to yourself and take a deep breath. Their cutting you off is out of your control, but how you react is in your control, and it is not worth risking serious injury or potentially your own life by getting into a confrontation with them.

Communication is always the key to dealing with difficult people, especially when it comes to one-on-one exchanges involving customer service, a rude employee at the DMV, etc. If you are on the business side of things, you need to be polite and professional at all times. Stay calm, collected, and focused on your job and allow them to get all of the issues out on the table before you address their concerns. Difficult people have the consistent need to demand that others listen to them. It may be hard not to intervene, but it is best to just let them spill out everything they have to say, and then you can proceed to help them out.

If you are on the opposite side of the business table, like trying to register your car at the DMV, you don't have to necessarily put your "professional face" on, but your "game face" is undoubtedly going to be useful and serve in your favor.

Remember to be polite, but you don't have to be a pushover. If the person handling your business is rude, impolite, or just difficult to deal with, feel free to ask to work with another individual or ask for their supervisor. You are giving them your business, and you should be treated with respect and dignity. If you are not, you need to speak up and demand it. You most certainly do not need to be rude to the individual by any means, but you do need to let them know that the way they are handling the situation is not adequate and you deserve to work with someone who is actually willing to help.

Dealing with difficult people is something that can be extremely trying on your mental state. When it comes down to it, you really just need to learn how to put your guard up a bit and process each situation as it arises. It is most certainly OK to choose not to deal with difficult people. Sometimes you just need to put a stop to things before they start to get out of hand. The more capable you are at figuring out how to deal with difficult people during difficult situations, the easier these things will start to come to you. It takes some time, patience, and a great deal of effort; however, once you start to figure out the process in its entirety, the easier it will start to come to you.

When you are successful at learning how to deal with difficult people, you will find that you will almost startle people who are difficult. This is the "kill them with kindness" philosophy. The more pleasant you tend to be and the more you can show a person that their behavior doesn't bother you in any way, shape, or form, the more you are proving to them that they can't get to you. Difficult people tend to feed on the negative energy of others—make sure that you don't give them the benefit of robbing you of your energy.

Make sure that when you come in contact with a difficult person you stay guarded, but as positive as you can be. When you keep your positive energy levels up, you are more able to process the difficult situation on a significantly more clear and concise level as well. This allows you to handle the situation more efficiently and effectively. Instead of becoming angry or shutting down emotionally and letting them have at you, put your guard up and hit them back with a force of positive energy. The more that you can control the situation, the easier it will be to effectively handle the situation and keep things in your favor.

As you start to learn how to handle difficult people, you need to be patient with yourself as well. Learning something new is a form of changing yourself, and that is something that is incredibly hard to do. As we change and grow, we learn how to adapt to different things in our lives, and that can play a role in how we deal with difficult people and difficult situations as well.

In life, we are surrounded by difficult people, and we encounter them on a daily basis. Make sure that you do not allow those individuals to frustrate you or steal your happiness. This, of course, is often easier said than done, but the more effort you put into bettering yourself and not lowering yourself to that person's level, the easier it will be to go about handling these individuals. While you may not be able to control how other people act, you can control how you react to them. This is the biggest thing you should keep in mind when you encounter a difficult person. Always be the bigger person, and don't give them the benefit of sinking down to their level.

If you can take the time to remind yourself that you are in a good place in your life and that the difficult person you are dealing with does not deserve to rob you of your mental well-being and energy, you are strengthening yourself and your own mental well-being. Practice this way of thinking, try to implement it when you are face-to-face with a difficult person, and put it to work for you. You will note that your whole perspective will start to change, and when you are faced with a difficult person or situation, you will feel as if it rolls off you like water runs off of a duck.

When you change your perspective, you are showing yourself that you are in control of the situation in its entirety and the difficult person does not have any control over you. You are taking back that control in order to save your own sanity and reduce your stress, and for peace of mind as well. One good thing that you can try to do is implement a mantra that can help bring you to a place of peace when you are dealing with a difficult person or situation. Some examples are as follows:

"I am safe. I am strong."
"I can handle anything."
"I am peaceful."
"I can do this."
"Just breathe."

Anything that is simple and easy to remember and that you can say to yourself when you are faced with a conflict will be helpful. Using a mantra is a great idea, but you can also opt to use visualizations. One that I have found that works quite well is to visualize a white light or bubble that surrounds you and protects you from the negative energy. Whenever you are faced with a difficult person or situation, envision whatever it is that you opted to utilize and imagine that you are surrounded by it in a manner that protects you from whatever is being thrown your way. When you use visualization, you are protecting yourself from difficult people and situations and ensuring that they can't get to you, harm you, or rob you of your energy and your good vibes.

The best offense is a good defense, and once you are better prepared to handle certain people and situations, you will start to find that it is actually quite easy—you need to be prepared for it from the start, though. In the following chapters, there are a number of excellent tips that you can take into consideration to help you prepare for those difficult people and situations so that you are ready and prepared to handle anything that gets thrown your way, no matter who or what is causing you that stress and hassle.

Make sure that you stick with it, stay positive, and keep learning all that you can in order to be at your best so that you can overcome any situation you are pressed with, including those involving difficult people. You may feel discouraged at times, and that is OK—you are literally retraining yourself to think in a completely different way—but stick with it. Don't get down on yourself. Change takes time, and the more you can look at this change as being something that is positive and highly beneficial to you, the easier it will be to accept and adapt.

Chapter 10
Coping Strategies for Dealing with Difficult People

Learning how to cope with difficult people in order to properly handle difficult situations can be an trying thing to accomplish. However, when you have the right tools under your belt, you can go about addressing people and certain situations with a sense of ease and confidence. When you understand the effective strategies that you can implement, they will be easier to effectively put into motion when the need arises. While some of the tips that are listed throughout this chapter are merely suggestions, they are excellent tactics that can get you started in learning how to address and deal with difficult people and help you implement your own personal strategies that work best for you.

There are a number of various strategies that can assist you when you are dealing with a difficult person. Regardless of who the person is, where you may find yourself in contact with them, or what the situation is, this chapter will provide some of the top coping mechanisms you can incorporate in order to successfully navigate the issue at hand. They will help you keep a positive sense of direction—and perhaps even an entirely different outlook about the situation as a whole.

When you come in contact with a difficult person or face a difficult situation, there are a number of emotions that you are going to experience, from anger and stress to feeling down, unmotivated, sad, or upset. You need to acknowledge whatever it is that you are feeling in order to understand what is happening and, in turn, allow it to pass. The more understanding you are about your emotions, the easier it will be for you to start to learn how to process them so you can gain control before they end up getting the best of you. Here are some really effective strategies that you may want to utilize when you are dealing with difficult people and trying situations:

Breathe. The first coping mechanism you'll want to implement is to take a deep breath. Taking a deep breath can be one of the quickest and easiest ways to regain your composure before addressing the situation. When you take the time to breathe deeply, you will find a sensation of balance throughout your body. The air fills up your lungs and travels throughout your body, and you end up exhaling that negative energy and removing it from your body. When you use proper and effective breathing techniques, you are successfully able to allow yourself the opportunity to process what is happening and work through it instead of allowing it to affect you. This gives you extra time to calmly gather and restore your peace of mind and your senses so that you can go about reacting properly.

Stay calm. It can be hard to stay calm under pressure. After taking deep breaths, you need to remain focused and keep reminding yourself to stay calm, as you don't know what you may have in store for you. In another chapter, we made note of the fact that choosing a mantra to recite when you are faced with a difficult situation can be a really great solution. It can help keep you calm during stressful times. Choose a mantra that is easy to remember—for example, "I am calm," "I can do this," or "I am stronger than I think I am"—and use it whenever the situation calls for it.

Be still. One of the biggest challenges you will face with regards to dealing with a difficult person is to resist the urge to put your guard up and even fight back. When we encounter a difficult person, we often find ourselves feeling threatened and our guard will instantly go up in order to protect ourselves. Unfortunately, that is one of the top things that will fire up a difficult person, and it often leads to much larger issues overall. If you encounter a difficult person, the first thing you will want to do is to "shut down" in a sense. It is totally acceptable to put your guard up and to protect your inner self by finding a sense of calm so you can be mindful of the situation at hand and how you need to proceed in order to downplay it, deal with it, or just walk away from it. Find that mindfulness and sense of being still so that you can decide what actions are going to be in your best interest and how you need to proceed from there.

When you are forced to deal with a difficult person, one thing that you need to make sure you do is listen to what the person is saying, free of judgement. All too often, difficult people are dealing with something that they are not able to process on their own, and it ends up coming across to those who are around them in a completely negative and irrational manner.

When you are able to meet that person with a clear and concise mindset, you not only prevent yourself from feeling attacked but also process through what that difficult individual is experiencing so as to not take it personally. When you find that you are capable of remaining calm and listening, it can also help you to process whether the person is trying to manipulate you in any way, shape, or form so you can ultimately protect yourself, if it comes down to it. When you come face-to-face with a difficult person, you are going to note that you most likely feel a little bit worn-out, tired, stressed-out, and overwhelmed. That is totally normal. The following are some things you can do when interacting with a difficult person:

Demand respect. Showing respect to someone who fails to show you respect is tough. However, when you show respect to a difficult person, you are taking the high road, and this is a great way to boost your confidence and show that person you are not a doormat. When you show respect, however, you need to demand it in return as well, and the more confidence you have, the easier it will be for those around you to see that.

This does not mean that you need to demand compliance; allow the person the chance to vent if they need to, but do not take it personally. Show them respect and demand it in return by setting your own limitations and boundaries. You are allowed to tell difficult people to not talk to you in a certain way. Respect is something that should come freely, and if you find that the person is not showing you respect even after you have made it known that you are deserving of it, you need to take the proper course of action to inform them that they aren't going to get whatever it is they want from you until they start to show you the respect you deserve.

Reflect and recharge. When you are done dealing with the difficult person, take some time to process and reflect upon what just happened. Confide in a trusted friend or family member, meditate, go for a run, or do yoga—anything that will help you take back the power that you lost in having to deal with that person. Don't hold your emotions in; your body is going to be fueled with adrenaline over the confrontation with that difficult person, and you need to make sure that you process and expel it in a healthy manner. Your first priority is you. Do not forget that!

These types of coping mechanisms and strategies are going to take you a bit of time to learn and practice before you regularly start to implement them when you are met with a difficult person or a stressful situation. The more you can practice them, the easier they will be to use when the time arises. Make sure that you try not to get discouraged with yourself if you find that you have tried some of these coping methods to no avail. It is going to take a little bit of time to unlearn the past behavior you have grown so accustomed to using over the years.

As you grow, you learn your own personal coping mechanisms for different situations. That is totally normal; however, some of those coping mechanisms and strategies are not healthy behavior, nor are they successful in proactively handling difficult people and difficult situations. You need to make sure that you are implementing the right tools so that you can successfully learn what strategies are going to work, which ones aren't going to work, and how you can modify others so they work for you. Stay positive and be sure to stick with it and not give up. The more positive you are about sticking with your new goals, the easier they will come to you and the likelier you will find success in dealing with difficult people in a beneficial and highly effective way.

As previously stated, learning how to effectively use coping strategies can take a tremendous amount of time, effort, and practice. However, the aforementioned tips can truly change your life when it comes down to being able to properly implement them during difficult times.

Difficult people are difficult for a reason: they do not know how to act during their own difficult situations, and all too often that leads to them lashing out at those around them. When you are able to utilize coping techniques as a means to get you through the difficult situation, you can learn how to talk the difficult person "down from the ledge" and potentially get them to a point where they can calm down and realize their lashing out has nothing to do with you.

Unfortunately, not all difficult people and difficult situations are the same. Knowledge and understanding are required to process the situation and to quickly figure out what steps are needed to resolve it and prevent it from getting out of hand and escalating even faster. In the next few chapters, we will be expanding upon this a little bit deeper in order to give you a new and improved perspective so that you can learn to process and properly handle any difficult situation or person, regardless of what it is.

Chapter 11
Quick-Thinking Strategies for Difficult Situations

In the last chapter we covered some of the top strategies that you can take advantage of when it comes to dealing with a difficult person. While those are undoubtedly the best ways to "train yourself" to effectively handle these people in your life, oftentimes we find ourselves in unexpected situations where we have no other option but to deal with a difficult person head-on.

When those issues arise, you more often than not are going to feel overwhelmed, and your brain will kick into a fight-or-flight response to protect you from harm, mental or physical. This means that you most likely will not be thinking clearly enough to utilize the aforementioned strategies. If that happens, there are some tips that you can quickly implement to handle the situation with grace, dignity, and sanity.

- **Listen.** One of the same techniques that you can utilize from the aforementioned chapter is to sit back and let the person just talk. Listen to what they have to say—let them vent. It is much the same as letting a child have a temper tantrum; allow the person to get whatever it is that they are trying to express out on the table and do not interrupt. This lets them relieve their issue and gives you a moment or two to process the situation and address it with a proper response. Listening to someone almost disarms them in a manner of speaking. When the person is able to get out their emotions, thoughts, and feelings and you, they will usually get over the issue now that the pressure has resolved. They just need to express what is bothering them to move past it, and by allowing them the opportunity to do that, you are actually helping them get through the issue easier and a lot faster as well.

- **Respond accordingly.** When you are ready, be sure not to respond in a manner that will escalate the situation. In situations that pertain to a difficult person who is fired up, you are going to want to say things like "I am going to resolve this" or "I apologize," depending on the situation. Your best bet is to utilize whatever statement works that will not escalate the situation. Do not mock them or act defensively toward the individual or the situation. You are also going to want to ensure that you try and avoid smiling, as this can often appear as if you are mocking the difficult individual. While humor can of course lighten the mood sometimes, this can quickly backfire if you are coming up against the wrong person. Make sure that you properly understand the situation, why it is currently escalating or has escalated, and then react accordingly. This is also where listening comes into play. You need to make sure that you understand where the individual is coming from.
- **Avoid anger.** The quickest way to de-escalate the issue is to prevent yourself from getting angry. All too often, and especially when it comes to being met with a sense of confrontation, people tend to raise their defenses in order to protect themselves (fight or flight). When you are coming up against someone whose anger is already growing, meeting that individual with anger is the

worst possible thing you can do, as this will only lead to a continuously escalating ordeal. When you meet anger with anger, no good can ever come from it. You need to stay calm and collected throughout the situation to ensure that you are addressing it with a clear head.

- **Keep space.** If you are dealing with a person who is angry, their anger is not being met with the answers, and you are seeing that their anger is only increasing, you are going to want to put distance between yourself and that individual. Anger rises quickly, and if you are in the wake of it you may end up in that individual's war path. Be sure to put physical distance between yourself and the difficult person in order to protect yourself, both mentally and physically. If you are dealing with a difficult person who is becoming increasingly angry, you need to make sure that you either walk away from that individual and let them handle their issue on their own, or you find someone else who can help you out in assisting the person. Sometimes personalities clash and it may be a better option to have someone else step in and take the reins from you to deescalate the situation as well.
- **Find help.** As previously stated, if you are involved in a confrontation with a difficult person, whether it is a family member or an angry customer, your best option is to find someone nearby to help. You may be feeling a bit overwhelmed with how the situation is going, and another individual might be able to help de-escalate the situation.
- **Trust yourself.** Always trust your gut instinct. If something does not feel right or seems to be elevating

a bit too quickly for your liking, it is OK to leave the situation and do what is right for you. Your gut instinct will never let you down with regards to the toughest issues, people, and situations. If you encounter a difficult person or a difficult situation and you start to get that unshakable feeling that something is not right, you need to take note of that feeling and run with it in order to save yourself from enduring the hardship of having to deal with a difficult person or situation.

While these are just a few good tips to use when met with an unexpected situation involving, it is of the utmost importance to keep in mind that every situation is different and you have to take things in stride. Your best bet is going to start with truly listening to what the person is saying in order to understand why they are upset or why they feel compelled to say the things that they do. Then you can better understand their frustration, anger, annoyance, or character flaws as a whole. This will allow you the opportunity to break down their emotions and react properly, while saving your sanity as well.

The more you implement these tips and strategies, the easier they will be able to work in your favor in dealing with difficult people, handling difficult situations, and possibly learning how to avoid difficult people and situations altogether. They will eventually become second nature.

Quick-thinking strategies can undoubtedly be arduous to accomplish when someone is in your face during a difficult situation. When people are angry, stressed-out, upset, etc., they are not going to process and hear what it is that you are trying to say to calm them down. When a difficult person is upset, they make the situation entirely about them, and you are likely going to be perceived as their enemy of sorts, even if you are trying to help. That is not a good feeling, and it can lead to a hard time processing the situation clearly, which can then lead to shutdown mode or even intense anger on your part as you feel threatened by the individual.

This is one of the biggest challenges when dealing with difficult people and difficult situations. Each one is going to be a different experience every time, no matter how well you know the person. In fact, it is even more difficult being able to learn how to effectively deal with individuals that you know quite well, because you think that you truly understand their character one day, and then the next it is entirely different. This is why learning the top strategies to be your best can ultimately teach others to be their best as well. We will be shedding more light on how to do just that in the next few chapters.

Chapter 12
Encouraging Yourself to Be Your Best

In this chapter, we will be exploring some of the top ways to be the best version of yourself. When you are at your best, you can have the confidence to do anything you put your mind to. You feel less inclined to fight battles that aren't worth your time. And you do not feel obligated to be around people who don' match your idea of what a genuinely decent human being is.

When you grow as an individual, you are learning to commit to self-love and unlocking a true sense of inner appreciation. This is something that many people tend to lack. We are all afflicted by things that take their toll on our lives and affect us in a negative manner. And this all too often can bring us down, which can lead to experiencing mental and physical issues. Those types of afflictions can build up so deeply within us that it truly is hard to break out of the cycle and find healing, inner peace, and genuine joy. But when you take the time to work on yourself, you are healing yourself from the inside out as well, and that can change your entire outlook on yourself and those around you.

Change is hard, and the process is a long and arduous journey, but it can be done. And when you reach the finish line, you will find that you are a remarkably better version of yourself, one who is stronger than ever before, one who is more apt to learn from their mistakes, and one who is continuously striving to better themselves as well. No one is perfect, but we can be the best version of ourselves. The best thing that you can do as you are on the journey of self-growth is to be completely patient with yourself and allow yourself the freedom to learn how to change while you grow.

When you are teaching yourself to change the habits that you have for so long relied upon because they are comfortable, you are going to need to be patient in order to allow for the opportunity to create the change you desire. Change is a huge deal, and many people feel they are failing again and again before they even start the process of becoming a successful individual, while a good majority of people tend to give up because change is difficult. There is nothing wrong with finding the process of internal change difficult, but when you are ready to take those steps, you need to proceed with a strong head and a good, positive attitude in order to truly find success in the long run. The more positive you stay, the easier it is to adapt to changes over time and to learn how to pick yourself up when you fall.

This leads us to the following questions: Where do you start and when is the right time to get started? Well, to put it simply, there is no better time than now to start working on improving yourself. The best way to get started is to take note of the fact that you are ready to make the changes necessary to become the very best version of yourself. Here are some of the top things you can do to take advantage of encouraging yourself to be your very best:

- **Think big.** When it comes to changing your outlook on life, you need to first start with your mind. Great minds think on a larger scale, and your thoughts go a long way in terms of determining the things you do and how you feel about yourself afterward. When you

are able to turn your way of thinking around and have a more positive outlook on life, you can achieve virtually anything you set your mind to, and this will ultimately lead to generating more positivity and success in your life.
- **Motivate yourself.** Motivation has a tremendous influence on you. When things fail to go as we plan, the only thing that can keep us going is to stay motivated until we reach our goals. Read some motivational quotes, listen to motivational speakers, and do what works for you to stay motivated.
- **Believe in yourself.** Believing in yourself is one of the most important things we can do for ourselves. When you believe that you can be the person that you want to be, you can be. Visualize yourself as a successful person and then do the things that are necessary to demonstrate that you are working toward bettering yourself. Try new things and believe that you are going to do great at them. When you walk around with poor self-esteem or believe that you are going to fail, you will fail, and you cannot possibly create any sort of positive change in your life.
- **Set goals.** Set a goal for everything that you do and aspire to do. This can help you become more determined and focused as a whole. Write down the goals that you want to achieve in a short amount of time and the goals you want to reach in the long term, and then tie them together. Place them in an area where you are sure to see them every day. When you set goals for yourself, you tend to hold yourself a lot more accountable than when you do not set goals. Think about how your short-term goals help you reach

your long-term goals as well. Goal setting is a great way to become a more positive person, and it will help bring out your best.

- **Plan accordingly.** We all need to learn how to plan our lives out properly and abide by a daily schedule in order to become more productive. It can be a tricky thing to accomplish, but avoiding menial tasks throughout the day can help you focus on your plans and goals. Remember to never take on more than you can handle. Learn time-management skills and ask for help when you need it. Planning your life accordingly is all about balance, and once you find that perfect middle ground, you will see success in virtually everything you do.
- **Seek new challenges.** You can find opportunity within the confines of failure. Never opt to avoid a challenge; on the contrary, look to challenges as excellent opportunities to push yourself while learning new things and learning from your mistakes as well. When you rise to any challenge that gets thrown in your path, you find strength in a way that you never thought was possible before. This truly is one of the best tips that you can take advantage of in order to learn from and grow into a stronger and more successful person overall.
- **Release your failures.** Failures that you've encountered in the past should never hold you back from taking risks in the future. You need to learn how to release memories of your past mistakes or else they will continue to hold you back in the future. Releasing your failures can be a tricky thing to learn if you have taught yourself for so long to hold onto them.

However, learning how to release those past failures can free your soul and lead to a lifelong feeling of inner peace. Learn how to release those past mistakes so that you can learn from them and ultimately grow as well.

- **Discover your strengths.** Similar to understanding what your weaknesses are and releasing your past failures, you also need to make sure that you take the time to figure out what your strengths are. The best way that you can learn how to be the best version of yourself is to find out what your strengths are and use them to your advantage. Get out of your comfort zone a little in order to figure out what your strengths are and how you can grow from them. You may end up surprising yourself with all of the remarkable things that you can do. Release that fear, spring forward, and figure out your limitless capabilities.

The journey of self-discovery can be a long and arduous one. However, when you are aware that certain troubles will arise, you can meet them as yet another challenge that you can learn and grow from. Roadblocks are most certainly inevitable, but when you learn how to tackle some of the issues that may come up, you can formulate the best course of action to overcome them. In this next section, we will be providing you with a few different examples of some roadblocks you may encounter on your journey to becoming the best possible version of yourself, and how you can rise above them.

- **Losing hope in your potential.** When we have thought badly about ourselves and our potential for such a long time, it can be hard to pull yourself out of that hole. When you find yourself dealing with negative thoughts about yourself and your capabilities, you need to give yourself some time to regroup and process your thoughts. Make a list of the things that you are the proudest of in your life—things you know you are great at—and read through it. Make sure you hang on to it so you can review it or add to it when you find yourself circling back to those thoughts of negativity.

- **Lack of courage.** We all struggle with bouts of dealing with a lack of courage at some point or another during our lives. This is an issue that can hit you quite hard when you are taking the steps to proactively change. A lack of courage is also one of the most common reasons why so many people give up on themselves. When you start to feel that your courage is slipping, take a mental note of what has led you to feel this way in the first place and then devise a plan of action to take the steps to do better. If you are feeling a bit overwhelmed for any reason, it is OK to take a few steps back to take the pressure off of yourself and go about reaching your goals in a different manner that may require a bit less effort than you were initially putting forth.
- **Fear of failure.** Fear is a difficult emotion that we all face at some point, and it is one of the trickiest things to learn how to overcome. Fear breeds negative energy in our minds, which can lead to outcomes that are not beneficial to your overall sense of well-being. Fear can lead you down a path where you want to give up on yourself and your goals, and it is nothing more than a complete waste of time. When fear enters your mind,

you need to attempt to identify the root cause of your fear and address it head-on. If you find that you cannot eliminate your fear on your own, do not be afraid to reach out to a trusted friend, family member, or professional counselor for guidance.

- **Inability or difficulty discovering your strengths.** All too often we are unable to uncover our own strengths—sometimes it is because we can't pinpoint what they are specifically, and sometimes it is because we don't think we have any. You may need to reach out to a trusted friend or family member to help you out with some ideas regarding what makes you such a remarkable person. Other people see us in an entirely different light, and just because we can't see something, does not mean that others can't. That is precisely why reaching out to someone whom you love and trust can really help you uncover all of your incredible strengths and talents.
- **Letting go of the old you.** If you have been implementing these tips, as well as some others that perhaps you picked up along the way, and you are not noticing any real change within yourself, you may have some issues with letting go of your past self and the bad habits that you had previously held onto. Remember to not get down on yourself; again, these things take time and a tremendous amount of effort. One of the best things you can do is keep pushing forward and working on yourself. Take the time to highlight your most recent successes and the positive developments and changes you have been working toward, and then compare those successes with the strategies you have utilized in the past—you are sure

to see noticeable improvements in your development as a whole.

As previously stated, working on improving yourself is one of the most difficult things that we, as humans, have to do. All too often we find ourselves getting stuck in an everyday routine, and this is exactly what happens to our character. We have for so long acted and reacted to things in one manner that when we try to break the habit, we are not always successful, especially the first few times we try to implement change. Do not be discouraged; the more you keep at it, the more you will find that things will start to become second nature, and you will begin to adapt to these new techniques with ease as you start the process of becoming a better version of yourself, which can lead you to helping others follow suit.

The key to learning how to be the best version of yourself is to understand that you are capable of accomplishing anything you want in your life. You can be the best version of yourself by acknowledging that while you may have certain flaws, you want to work on them in order to improve who you are as a person. When we acknowledge our faults and understand that we are not perfect, we can then take the proper steps that are required to transform into the person that we really want to be. Transformation is not an easy thing to do. Better yourself, and better those around you!

Remember that in order to be the best version of yourself, you need to be proud of who you are, and you need to fall in love with yourself as well. Acknowledge all of the things that make you great, write down a list of them, and keep adding to it, especially as you start to grow, change, and evolve into the best version of yourself. You are going to change, you are going to grow, and you can find success in becoming a new and amazing individual. Do not get discouraged with yourself; stay positive, focused, and driven, and stick with the belief that you are going to make some remarkable changes in your life in order to become the incredible human being that you are.

Another thing you'll want to do is keep updating your goals as you start to reach them. If you have reached your goal, make a new one, or if you are not reaching your goals in a timely or successful manner, change them up a little bit so that you can more easily reach them and experience success. There is absolutely nothing wrong with changing your existing goals and updating them to allow you the opportunity to be more successful in reaching them. The ultimate goal is to reach your end goal, so why not change things up if your regular plan of action just is not going to work out like you thought it would? If you stay positive, focused, and encouraged, you will find that you can become a remarkable version of yourself in a timely and successful manner.

Chapter 13
Encouraging Others to Be Their Best

In this chapter, we will provide you with some tips on how you can encourage others to be their best as well. This is very important because when you are at your best, those around you will want to be their best too, and this can be incredibly helpful when it comes to dealing with difficult individuals you encounter.

Trying to encourage someone to be their best and much less negative can be difficult. You need to make sure that you are patient with the difficult person and do not come off as if you are blatantly trying to change them. Make sure that if you approach someone to encourage them to be their best, you do so with a sense of grace, dignity, and positivity. Be gentle with the individual; you never know what someone is going through or what makes them act so difficult. You do not need to come at someone and point out that they are being difficult. There are various things that you can do to silently encourage them to become a better person. Consider trying the following:

- **Be an example.** In order to truly be a leader and inspire others to be their best, you need to learn how to lead by example. In order to accomplish this, you need not only the courage and confidence to act when needed but also the ability to remain flexible and persistent while practicing a sense of genuine authenticity in every aspect of your life. You also need to allow them the opportunity to rise up to their greatest potential without trying to micromanage them. The more that you can be a positive, shining light in the lives of those people who surround you, the more they will want to be like that as well. You are encouraging others to become better because they want a little bit of what it is that you have. Be happy, be positive, and be bright, and others will want to follow suit.

- **Set realistic goals and expectations.** Make sure that you don't settle for the "good enough" standard. Be sure that you are always setting your personal standards to a higher standard, and those around you will, in turn, follow your example. Set realistic expectations and goals without implementing unreasonable demands, and make time for people to come to you with feedback about how things are going, how things could be changed or improved, etc. When you set realistic goals and expectations for those around you when you need to accomplish something, you are giving them something to strive to attain that is actually within their reach and capability. This is a positive, motivating step for that difficult individual, and it can give them the opportunity to take pride in accomplishing those goals, thus leading to a potentially happier and prouder individual, as opposed to a negative, difficult one. People thrive on accomplishments and successes, and when you can help someone, even a difficult individual, reach their goals, you can help that person become much happier as well.

- **Become a master of empathy.** Do not assume that you know what those around you want or how they think. When you are able to utilize empathy, you can then begin to understand what those around you truly want and expect out of a situation. Whether it involves family members or coworkers, empathy goes a long way when it comes to understanding the perspective of someone else, especially people who are difficult. The more you can practice empathy, the more confident you will become in your communication skills. This can help you learn how to smooth out difficult situations regardless of who is involved in them. Empathy is one of the most important things that you can have in terms of dealing with difficult people. When you are empathetic, you are able to get down to the difficult person's level and see why they are acting that certain way in the first place. When you can express empathy, you can reach out to the difficult person and let them know that you genuinely care and want to assist them in whatever it is they are dealing with. Empathy helps you create connections with those around you, and it is one of the best things that you can do to help a difficult person grow and become the best version of themselves in the long run.
- **Build relationships with others.** Being self-sufficient is an important asset; however, formulating relationships is of equal importance. Difficult people often coerce or force others to be around them instead of letting relationships grow naturally. Use that as an example of what not to do. Build quality relationships with those around you by creating a foundation that is built upon a sense of mutual respect and trust.

Approach people with curiosity about the things that genuinely interest them, ask questions about who they are and what they believe, and build upon that relationship from there. This type of collaboration, in turn, formulates a basis of mutual understanding on how to inspire each other, and that leads to inspiring others as well. Building relationships, especially with difficult people, is hard to do, but it can be done if you have the patience and care to do so. Make sure that you are ready to deal with a difficult person and all of the flaws, difficulties, and challenges regarding their personality. If you are not, they will end up stealing your energy and only creating more stress and hardships for you overall.

- **Trust the process.** It is important to continue working on bettering yourself and trusting the entire process as a whole. Keep working to reach your personal and professional goals, and help others to reach theirs as well. Even though you are working on yourself, the best way to inspire others is to support them and lift them up as well. Ask questions about the things that are most important to them and what their goals are. Then share ideas of some goal-setting tips that you have found personally helpful. When you are able to demonstrate a mutual respect for everyone who is involved in your life, difficult or not, the process of collaboration can lead to inspiration in its entirety.

It is important to understand that although we can strive to do our best and encourage others to do the same, not everyone wants to "be fixed," and that is OK. It's also something that we need to be OK with too. This is largely the case with regards to dealing with difficult people. More often than not, difficult people do not see any issue with how they act or how they ultimately treat those around them, and if they fail to see an issue, they are not going to see you are trying to help them or listen to any advice that you have to offer.

Difficult people tend to shut down when others offer them constructive criticism or tips on how they can be more successful. Again, that is perfectly OK, but you need to be sure that you give them some space and allow them to be as they are. You can't fix someone who fails to think they are broken, and it is in your best interest to simply let them go on about their lives however they see fit, whether you agree with them or not. This is not to say, however, that you need to sit back and allow a difficult person to direct any sort of harm toward you or those around you.

If it becomes necessary, it is of the utmost importance to speak up and tell the difficult person that enough is enough, and they need to stop treating you and those around you in the manner that they are. There is no need to have to put up with mental stress or any sort of harm simply because that difficult person in your life fails to see how bad they are treating you, or those around you. You need to speak up for yourself, as well as for those who can't or are unwilling to, and put an end to the hassle or abuse.

Dealing with difficult people is easily one of the hardest things that we have to do in our lives. It is not fun, and each situation is different, regardless of who it is that you are dealing with. If difficult people are not willing to change themselves or better themselves, that is their own fault, not yours. Keep working on yourself, and remember to not let anyone bring you down, no matter who it is. Even if you do not think that you are inspiring someone to be a better version of themselves, you are taking back your own power by not letting it personally affect you, while also taking the necessary steps to improve yourself.

Make sure that you stay positive when you are attempting to encourage a difficult person to be their best. Remember that change is hard. You are working on yourself as well, so you know just how hard it is to improve. Keep motivating them, keep encouraging them, and maintain a positive attitude about the entire experience. The more motivating and encouraging you can be, the more people will really want to work on improving themselves and creating some positive and beneficial change within themselves as well.

Chapter 14
Understanding Trauma

Trauma is something that few people tend to understand when it comes to dealing with emotional responses. The vast majority of people who hear the term *trauma* assume it means some type of physical harm, such as an injury related to an accident, or it refers to problems that stem from deeper, darker mental issues such as abuse. However, trauma can stem from things such as a buildup of stress that your body and mind are not capable of processing. In this chapter, we will be exploring just what exactly trauma is, how it affects your body and mind, and how dealing with difficult people and situations can actually lead to trauma without you even knowing that it is happening.

To begin, it is imperative to understand what the term *trauma* means in both an emotional and a psychological sense. More often than not emotional and psychological trauma result from overly stressful situations that can ultimately shatter your overall sense of security and well-being, thus creating a feeling that you are completely helpless in a world that is fueled by danger. Psychological and emotional traumas can leave you with conflicting and intense feelings that you can't process, memories that hinder your ability to move forward, and a sense of anxiety that will not leave you alone.

Trauma can be a buildup of numerous things that keep bombarding you, wearing you down, and causing you to experience stress, emotional pain, and feelings that are just too unbearable for you to handle on your own. Trauma can build up when we least expect it, because it slowly creeps in on us and takes its toll on our mind and mental state. In turn, it can affect our bodies as well, and we may not even know that it is happening to us.

Harmful or even life-threatening events, including dealing with difficult people, can lead to your brain triggering a release of adrenaline, which then activates your "fight, flight, or freeze" response. When your brain senses that you are in danger, it kicks into gear to get you out of whatever the situation is in order to protect you.

Even when traumatic experiences go unresolved, they can stimulate the fight, flight, or freeze response during situations that are non-threatening. When you experience trauma, particularly during your childhood, your brain structure can actually change, and this can contribute to long-term behavioral and physical health problems.

People tend to develop coping mechanisms in order to take the sting out of the pain trauma causes. Some of these coping mechanisms can be classified as "health-risk behaviors," which include overeating, eating unhealthy foods, tobacco use, substance abuse, and risky sexual activity. When traumatic stress is left untreated, coping mechanisms can lead to different types of issues such as depression, social isolation, anxiety, and even chronic diseases such as cancer, diabetes, substance-use disorders, and hypertension.

Living with trauma can lead to having to deal with lifelong health problems as well. Some of these health-related problems can include chronic heart and lung diseases, liver disease and liver cancer, viral hepatitis, sexually transmitted infections, autoimmune diseases, depression, anxiety, and various mental health conditions.

Childhood trauma is something that needs to be noted here because it can lead to the inability to handle and resolve difficult situations and difficult people. When you experience trauma as a child, that buildup in your head can put a complete block on you being able to process your emotions properly as an adult. Let's take a look at a couple of examples of how childhood trauma can lead to the inability to process your emotions during difficult situations.

I once sat down and talked to a young woman who was dealing with social anxiety and depression, and she was struggling to figure out why it seemed that these issues were simply coming out of the woodwork. She claimed that her feelings seemed to be increasing over the years and only getting worse and more difficult to process. I asked her what her childhood was like, and I was stunned with some of the stories she had to tell once she began to open up past the initial "Oh, it was fine."

The vast majority of her childhood memories stemmed from issues that related to her parents constant fighting, marital infidelity, and emotional abuse. She had a lot of really good stories to tell in terms of spending time with either just her mother, or just her father, but never both of them together. Her parents had a lot of disdain for one another, and they were staying together purely for her and her older brothers.

These painful childhood memories began at such a young age that she started to push away her own emotions over the years to a point that whenever she was faced with any sort of conflict, she would shut down completely. This led to her becoming a victim of sexual abuse, physical abuse, and mental abuse from a multitude of partners she strived to obtain a sense of safety from. And this led to a downhill spiral effect that ended with her struggling to deal with her current pressing issues of social anxiety and depression, all because of childhood trauma that she had learned to no longer think about and had pushed out of her mind so she could simply go through the day with a fake smile on her face.

Unfortunately, her job required her to deal with difficult coworkers and clients on a regular basis. She learned how to repress her emotions each and every day, and was all too often the "go-to" person to get yelled out for not doing her job right or for a customer to lash out at due to product-related issues. She was burned out and emotionally spent, and she was completely unable to process why she was feeling the way she was. She could not understand that her issues of childhood trauma had built up so heavily in her mind that she was now unable to cope with and properly handle difficult people and difficult situations.

I was able to share some of my relevant experiences with her on the subject and encouraged her to seek some help in the form of professional counseling. Unfortunately, I have not spoken to her since that day, but I most certainly hope that she has sought help and is on the path of internal healing from her pain. I also hope she knows that she does not have to live her life through the pain of the past any longer, and there is hope that she can find true, inner healing that will assist her in being able to properly handle difficult people and situations, which can ultimately benefit her overall mental health and well-being. And I hope *you* know that too.

There is hope through healing, and the very first step is to start the process of reflecting on your past trauma so that you can better understand why you are the person you are today. We all have experienced some form of trauma in our lives that could be related to many different things, including family issues, eating disorders, or bad breakups in high school, to list but a few. Trauma comes up when we least expect it, and all too often we simply push it out of our heads and just learn how to deal with it instead of taking the time to evaluate it and then heal from it.

So that brings us to the following questions: How do you confront issues that are related to trauma that may have occurred years ago or just recently, and how do you learn to heal from that trauma in order to heal yourself and progress and grow as a person? The first thing you need to do is understand and accept that you have been affected by issues that have led you to experiencing trauma. Once you understand what trauma truly is, how it affects you, and that you are experiencing it, you can then accept that you need to start taking the following steps to fix the issue and start the healing process:

- **Acknowledgement.** First and foremost, you need to acknowledge the fact that trauma is affecting who you are and how you react to certain circumstances, particularly those related to dealing with difficult people and difficult situations. When you acknowledge that your life has been heavily affected by issues of past trauma, you can then take the necessary steps to regain control of your life and work on addressing the pain that has been holding you down.
- **Acceptance.** Next, you need to accept the fact that trauma is holding you down. Acceptance is different than simply acknowledging trauma, as you can only begin the process of true emotional healing by accepting the fact that you are being afflicted by

trauma. It does not matter where that trauma is stemming from; it is taking its toll on your life, and you need to take back your power to begin the healing process in order to grow as a person. Accept your trauma, and then make sure that you take the proper measures to work on dealing with it and moving forward from it.

- **Reflection.** Now is when you take the time to sit back and reflect upon some of the past issues that have led you to experience the trauma that is bogging you down. When we take the time to reflect, we can sort through the traumatic events and then process them accordingly in a healthy manner. One of the best ways to reflect upon our past or present traumatic events is to write them down. Think back to your earliest memory of when you first started to make note of the fact that you simply were just not feeling right, and then write down that personal experience or event on paper or in a journal. More of your memories will begin to surface the more you are able to reach into your brain's memories. You really need to keep in mind that reflecting on past trauma is going to release a lot of personal emotions for you, and you need to make sure that you are ready for it. Unlocking trauma is going to unleash a whirlwind of emotions, so you really need to make sure that you have a support person, or support persons, in place to help you out and talk you through your pain in order to move past it, especially if you find that you just are not quite ready to deal with the emotions at the time that they start to flow. Healing is a process that takes a tremendous amount of time and devotion. It is OK to find that sometimes you just are not ready to deal with things. Go at your own pace and trust the process.

- **Process.** The brain works in a number of mysterious ways, and trauma has a way of shoving painful memories into the back of your brain so that you simply do not have to deal with them. Keep digging at these thoughts in order to start bringing them to the surface so that you can sort through them and begin the journey of healing. When you are able to pull as many of these painful issues of past trauma to the surface, you will experience new levels of the healing process. And processing through these painful emotions is the best way to start the process of healing in its entirety. Again, it should be reiterated that healing from personal trauma is a time-consuming process, and it is most certainly something that is going to take time, energy, and dedication to fully accomplish. Trust the process and go with the flow of your emotions. Everything that you go through is exactly where you need to be.
- **Healing.** When you are ready to start the journey of healing, you should come to understand that you simply do not need to be alone in the process. The journey of healing is a long and arduous one, particularly when it comes to healing from issues that are related to past trauma. You never know what sort of memory is going to come up and flood you with a total lack of control. Whether you seek the assistance of a trusted friend, family member, or

professional counselor to aid you in dealing with some of your emotions, there are a number of different options for you to get started on the process of finding total healing for the mind, body, and soul.
- **Evolve and grow.** With healing comes growth and a sense of the evolution of who you are as an individual. This is the biggest step you can take when it comes down to dealing with issues that are related to trauma, and this evolution and growth are the very beginnings of opening the doors to being able to learn how to cope with and properly handle difficult people and difficult situations. The healthier you are in terms of your mental and physical well-being, the more apt you are to successfully handle any situation, regardless of how difficult it may be.

Traumatic experiences do not have to weigh you down, nor do they have to take their toll on who you are as a person today. And they most certainly do not have to affect the way that you respond to difficult people and difficult situations.

When you are able to take the proper steps needed to realize that you are suffering from past trauma, and that you are ready to finally begin the journey of emotional healing, you will find that you are also emotionally ready to respond to difficult people in a healthy manner, and in a manner which no longer affects you personally.

The time has finally come where you take back the power and pain of your past in order to successfully create a better and stronger version of yourself for a stress-free and pain-free future that is also free of trauma.

Chapter 15
Healing Yourself

Dealing with difficult people and difficult situations is incredibly trying on one's mental health. While we covered long-term coping strategies in one of the previous chapters, here we will be exploring one of the biggest things that you can do to make sure you are always prepared to deal with difficult people, and that is to make sure that you are taking care of yourself first and foremost. Your own mental health and overall sense of well-being affects how you are able to successfully handle certain difficult situations. Here we will be providing you with some ways that you can take advantage of healing yourself on an emotional level in order to properly and powerfully handle difficult people and situations.

Being able to handle difficult situations and people is hard to do for anyone, but the more mentally grounded and stable you are, the more balanced you are as a whole, and that can help you to handle those situations with ease and a better sense of stability. So, what can you do? The first thing is to understand that you need to put yourself first. If your own mental state is not as healthy as it can possibly be, then you won't be able to deal with those who are around you, most notably difficult people. Here are some ways that you can put yourself first in order to find a sense of balance, well-being, and healing:

- **Work out.** One of the best ways to go about learning how to heal yourself mentally is to work on yourself physically. When your body feels good about itself, your mental health will play into that as well. Our bodies and minds are entirely hardwired and connected. They literally go hand in hand, so if you are mentally stressed-out to the max, your body is going to feed off of that, and you are not going to perform at your max capacity either. Cardio sports like boxing, martial arts, and running are all awesome ways to cut loose and lose yourself in your workout, but they also are not for everyone. If cardio is not your thing, try some lower key types of physical activities such as yoga, Pilates, or just taking a nice stroll before work, after work, or on your lunch break! The more you are able to get out there and get your heart rate up, the better you are going to feel overall, both mentally and physically.

- **Take advantage of "me time."** Again, there is no shame in putting yourself first, especially if you work in situations where you are constantly having to deal with difficult people or situations, or your home life is a bit difficult as well. Regardless of your difficult situation, do not ever feel ashamed about putting yourself first. Get home, take a hot bath or shower to rinse away the stress of the day, do your workout, have a glass of wine, and just veg out for a bit watching your favorite shows. Whatever is a healthy strategy (and by healthy I mean not overdoing it with regards to losing yourself, having too much to drink, etc.) to just chill out for a bit and take a moment for yourself once during the day.

- **Try meditation.** Meditation is something that requires focus, dedication, and a tremendous amount of patience; however, being able to do it can unlock a world of newfound stress relief, inner peace, and mindfulness. If you are unfamiliar with the world of meditation, you may want to try out a guided meditation via YouTube or a podcast. Guided meditations assist you in learning the art of meditation without having to stress yourself out about the fact that your thoughts keep coming and you just can't seem to focus. When you have a bit of meditation practice under your belt, you can give it a shot on your own. Sometimes using something that you can focus on, like a candle, can really help you clear your thoughts, direct your focus, and really unlock the core benefits that come from successful meditation.
- **Do not be hard on yourself.** One of the most difficult things that we unknowingly do is put too much pressure on ourselves. We work hard, stress out, and have a multitude of complex things that hit us every single day that can all too often make us feel defeated, like we are not doing our best, and like we simply are just not worthy. When these thoughts come up—trust me, they always seem to come at the worst possible time—it can be hard to push past them and keep moving forward. Sometimes you need to just sit with your thoughts, think about what is happening that is making you feel how you are, and then allow those thoughts to pass. As hard as it may seem, the more you can push those thoughts out of your mind and tell

yourself you are doing the very best that you possibly can, the better you will find you can react more successfully to difficult situations and people.

Your mental health is something that can be a bit difficult to cope with at times, particularly if you are constantly having to deal with difficult people on a regular basis. However, mental health is of the utmost importance, and you need to make it a priority to keep yours in good shape. Whether you opt to eat better, quit a bad habit, take up yoga or running, or start taking a hot bath after a long and stressful day, ensure that you are taking the time for yourself in order to promote and balance your internal and mental well-being as well as your overall health.

So many people struggle with mental health issues, and if too often you feel like you are on the verge of a mental collapse or breakdown due to difficult people or difficult situations, you need to make sure that you are taking the time to analyze and process what is happening. When you are able to understand that you are struggling with an issue, you can then learn how to properly deal with it.

You also need to understand that it is more than OK to accept that you are not OK, and to also take whatever action is necessary, such as counseling, to help make yourself feel better. If running and a change of diet is not doing it for you, find something that makes you feel good. And as previously stated, if you are feeling like you are not capable of handling so much on your own, be sure to reach out to a professional for some added tips and guidance that you can implement in order to help heal yourself.

You should always be your number one priority. If you are not feeling good about yourself, those around you can't feel good about themselves either. Take the time to find the healing that you need in order to restore your own sense of balance, harmony, and well-being, and then you can take back the power to share your inner light and grace with everyone you come in contact with.

Conclusion

We are always going to encounter difficult people and difficult situations in our day-to-day lives. And while these people and times can be undoubtedly trying and hard to cope with, when you have the tools and techniques to handle them properly, you will find that you are able to control the things that seemed out of your control before.

Being able to learn and incorporate the correct techniques that can be used in your favor to properly handle difficult people and diffuse virtually any difficult situation that you may find yourself in can be one of the most powerful things you can do for yourself. Having this sort of power will give you the confidence to know that you can control any situation that gets thrown your way.

The process of self-growth is a hard, long, and arduous journey that takes time and a ton of commitment to accomplish. As is the case with virtually anything you seek to do in your life, you need to be ready to take the necessary steps and action to succeed. And it should be noted that the biggest key that you need to unlock the door to properly being able to handle those difficult people in your life is to simply put yourself first and work on you. The better you are mentally, the more prepared you will ultimately be to tackle difficult situations with ease and a sense of confidence when they arise. This is a great way for difficult people to see that you are not an easily manipulated person, and they will quickly back off when they realize they are not going to be able to push your buttons and make you angry or upset.

Be strong and believe in yourself and your abilities. Growth takes patience and acceptance of who you are and what your capabilities are as a whole. The best way to grow is to take the first step and then just keep moving forward. Keep in mind that slip-ups can and will occur, especially when our patience is tested by difficult people. That is OK, but it is important to remember you need to get right back to work by utilizing the strategies and tips that can be found throughout the pages of this book. Stay positive, stay motivated, and be confident in yourself, and strategically being able to handle difficult people will end up becoming second nature to you.

The following quote has stuck with me since I read it, and you may want to keep it in mind during situations that call for having to deal with difficult people: "Agreeing to things just to keep the peace is actually a trauma response. When you do this, you are disrespecting your boundaries. No more making yourself uncomfortable for others to feel comfortable. You have control now. You run your life. Take up space and use your voice."

As you may remember from an earlier chapter on the subject, trauma is something that can build up within your mind and body without you actually even being able to truly comprehend what is happening to you. Trauma is not necessarily physical trauma, which is often the main thing that people think about when they hear the term *trauma*. Trauma can stem from a number of different things, and when you are feeling overly stressed and beaten down, it is of the utmost importance to understand that trauma has the potential to set in. But trauma does not need to control your life, and when you understand how the process of trauma actually works, you can take note of it and even assist others and encourage them to get the help that they need to heal and grow.

When you are able to successfully assist difficult people by politely letting them know that their nature is weighing on you and those around you, you will find that you are more capable of handling difficult people on a much larger scale. The process of being able to study people who are difficult to get along with is a great way to learn their idiosyncrasies. Then you can decide to live with them, help them change or heal, or keep yourself away from them for your own mental sanity and overall sense of well-being.

Be sure to always take the time to reflect on the things that are important to you at the end of each day. When you take the time to count your blessings and reflect on what is important to you, you can save yourself a tremendous amount of stress and the hassle of dealing with difficult people who just are not worth your time and energy. You need to remember to put your own mental state first and foremost, and never let people rob you of your mental health simply due to their own difficult actions and intentions. You are worth keeping yourself safe and sound, both mentally and physically.

Stress can wreak havoc on your body, and if your stress is being caused by a difficult person, you need to make sure that you bring this to their attention in order to protect yourself from that person if they are unwilling to change. When you offer your help, assistance, and support to someone who only shrugs it off, you need to ensure that you do not waste your time and energy until they are willing to make some changes to their difficult behavior. Remain true to yourself; you can only provide support to difficult people for so long before it really starts to weigh on you, and sacrificing your personal health and well-being just is not worth it.

Dealing with difficult people is hard, but you need to remember that you are always going to come in contact with them. However, when you have the proper tools to deal with difficult people and difficult situations, you will find that you can effectively diffuse any situation with ease and success. Make sure that you stay as positive as you can in any situation, and remain true to yourself and who you are. If you do those things, you will find that you can handle anything or anyone in an effective manner.

To put it simply, remain true to yourself and you can tackle anything.

Made in the USA
Middletown, DE
11 December 2021